Endorsements

A whirlwind study of nine women in the Bible by an author who understands not only the text but how these stories apply to the present and the future. Lisa Radcliff's expertise as a mental health coach helps her to see how these gripping stories from Scripture help us grow in grace and depend on the Lord with all our hearts. Read this book and I assure you that you will be greatly helped.

Derek W. H. Thomas, senior minister, First Presbyterian Church, Columbia SC (retired), Chancellor's Professor, Reformed Theological Seminary, teaching fellow, Ligonier Ministries

We, as women who have been hurt by sexual abuse, need and want healing. Lisa Radcliff has a gift of compassion for women who have been hurt, and she expresses that through this book. Lisa has taken women from the Bible who have been hurt and has by grace delivered her own heartfelt message to those who need to hear healing through these women's stories. Lisa not only has a loving, committed heart for women who have been hurt through sexual abuse, she also has a heart that strives to follow God and His word. I am grateful that God brought Lisa across my life path.

Leah Powley, founder, Learning to Breathe Again, a support group for women who have suffered sexual abuse, Certified Master Mental Health Coach

Lisa Radcliff, she delivers a powerful account of God's enduring love through the traumas and tragedies of life. She looks at various women in the Bible, that faced a great deal of trauma and tragedy, tells their story and parallels this to many women today. We find strength, hope, and God's love in the pages of her book. Lisa's book is arranged so that we are able to read it independently or share the journey with those ladies in our lives.

Lisa has been a speaker for Women of Hope, where she was able through her inspirational way and humor, reach women to let them know, they are not alone, that they are loved by the one true living king Jesus, and that God is for us.

Tara Freeman, founder of Women of Hope

Lisa Radcliff clearly has something important to say. She has a story to tell, and in many ways it's a story that few are willing to tell, using some of the least-told narratives in Scripture. But it's an important story that brings healing. And further, she does so in a way that grabs your attention and holds it: not just intellectually but deep down inside. May God use her faithfulness to restore bruised souls and enlighten Christ's church.

> **Ronald L. Kohl**, senior pastor, Grace Bible Fellowship Church, Quakertown, Pennsylvania

Without exception, this book is a beacon of hope for women who have experienced sexual abuse and trauma. It powerfully affirms that God is for you—even in the midst of brokenness, shame, and silence. Through its pages, readers will see how God can redeem even the darkest moments and use them to uplift and encourage others. This book beautifully connects the personal stories of today's women with those of women in the Bible, showing that God's love is unwavering, no matter your past. A must-read for anyone seeking healing, restoration, and renewed purpose.

> **Terry S. Derstine**, founder of Sweatshirt of Hope

I've known Lisa Radcliff since we were classmates in junior high and high school. My own faith journey began at age 16, largely due to Lisa's influence during that pivotal time in my life, and I've been walking with the Lord ever since.

As a life coach, former pastor's wife, and a survivor of sexual abuse, I can say with deep conviction that This I Know . . . is a book whose time has long been overdue. I'm so grateful that time has finally come.

In all my years in Christian ministry—especially as a youth pastor's wife—I have seen firsthand how rarely this topic is addressed in a way that is both biblically grounded and deeply compassionate. Lisa brings both. Her knowledge of Scripture is profound, but what makes this book truly remarkable is the warmth and care that radiates from her pen as she walks us through these painful yet powerful stories of women in the Bible.

This book is not just for survivors—it's for anyone wondering where God is in the midst of sexual trauma, in a world (and yes, even in the church) where this issue is far too common. Lisa helps us see God's heart: how He sees us, loves us, and walks with us, even in our most painful places.

If you're feeling hesitant to read a book on this topic, I understand—it's normal to feel a little afraid. But if you're looking for healing, growth, or simply a better understanding of how to help others, *God is for Me. . .* is a safe and grace-filled guide. Lisa handles this sensitive subject with such tenderness and truth that you'll feel seen, supported, and ultimately, more deeply connected to God's love.

Amy Scott, certified life coach

God is for Me is a profound and courageous work. By tenderly exploring the stories of women in the Bible who suffered sexual harm, it reveals God's unwavering heart for the broken. This book offers both biblical depth and gentle hope, showing readers that God truly sees, loves, and restores.

Robyn Dykstra, national Christian speaker, author, and professional speech coach

When the world is silent, and often careless towards those who have experienced sexual harm, God speaks up! His heart of love is revealed to these nine women in Scripture, who indeed, suffered some form of sexual harm. He speaks: you matter, you have value and worth, and purpose still in my kingdom. In *God is for Me: A Biblical Character Study of God's Heart for the Sexually Harmed*, Lisa showcases God's love and concern and offers a thought-provoking study that will help on the healing journey. Lisa also speaks up to ensure the safety of our children through the importance of enacting polices and awareness in our communities wherever children could be at risk of sexual harm.

Leslie H., abuse survivor

A masterful treatise on God's heart for all victims! This study meets a deep need in the church, brought together by the four remarkable strengths Lisa offers: unwavering biblical fidelity, personal and professional wisdom, a deep compassion for victims, and a concise, practical framework for care. This book is a much-needed gift to the church. Highly recommended!

David Matchette, senior pastor, Cornerstone Church of Skippack

Every survivor's path toward healing is as varied as the individual. Yet, within the heart of every Jesus follower who has experienced sexual harm echoes the same wounding statement and valid question, "This was my fault." "God, where were you?" Scripture has much to say about God's heart for those who have been abused. Lisa knows this. Allow her to walk with you as you study the women in scripture who survived as well.

Carolyn Ruch, steward, Rise and Shine Movement

Sexual abuse is unfortunately rampant within society. It is also all too frequently found within Christian circles. Oftentimes, the Bible is not seen as a book that speaks to those who have experienced such trauma. In this book, experienced author and speaker Lisa Radcliff explores the stories of nine women who have experienced abuse. Her insights from one who has experienced such pain will provide an important resource for those dealing with the scars of the past and insight for those wanting to help those who have experienced such harm.

Dr. Drake Williams, minister of mission and theology, Central Schwenkfelder Church, Worcester, Pennsylvania

God is for Me is a powerful and compassionate guide for women who have survived sexual abuse and have wrestled with the haunting thoughts, "Where was God? Why did He let this happen? Can He still use me?". The author's book gently steps into that sacred space with honesty, compassion, and truth. *God is for Me* is more than a Bible study; it's a healing encounter with God's heart through the stories of women in Scripture who were wounded, violated, and discarded by others, but never abandoned by God.

Page by page, it reveals a God who never looks away from suffering, and who refuses to let abuse be the final word over your life. This book speaks directly to survivors who want more than healing; they want to know what God says about their pain, their worth, and their future. If you are longing for proof that God was there, that He still is, and that your story is not too broken for Him to redeem, this book will meet you with truth that is as gentle as it is powerful. You are not forgotten. You are not alone. And you are not beyond God's purpose.

Cindy S., abuse survivor

While our culture and our churches often hides stories of sexual abuse, the Bible talks about them, and so does Lisa Radcliff. Radcliff not only sheds light on these dark stories, but she also offers words of comfort, hope, and healing to victims and survivors, and to any of us who know and care for those who have been harmed. Ultimately, she helps all of us connect to a God who comes alongside people in suffering.

David T. Lamb, MacRae Professor of Old Testament, dean of the faculty, Missio Seminary, author of *God Behaving Badly, 1-2 Kings* (Story of God), and *The Emotions of God*

This book meets a deep and often unmet need. It amplifies and rightly names the stories in Scripture that reflect the realities of sexual abuse and exploitation—stories too often overlooked or sanitized. In doing so, it offers a lifeline to survivors, helping them see their own pain reflected in the biblical narrative and, more importantly, introducing them to the God who sees, knows, and longs to meet them in their suffering. It is also a prophetic warning and urgent message to the Church, calling us to recognize the crucial role our response plays in either furthering harm or fostering healing

Dr. Heather Evans, LCSW, Evans Counseling Services, LLC, Voices of Survivors Project, Understanding Complex Trauma and Posttraumatic Growth in Sex Trafficking Survivors

This book is for both survivors of sexual harm and those who have ever been perplexed about how the stories in the Bible that describe sexual harm could ever be anything other than tragic stories to skim through quickly on the way to happier passages.

Lisa skillfully explains these stories using the language of sexual trauma that we understand today while still being faithful to Scripture. She reveals how these hard parts of Scripture show God's heart of love for survivors of sexual harm.

Rachel Schmoyer, pastor's wife, author of *Take it to Heart: 30 Days Through Revelation*

I am deeply grateful for this book! Lisa and I have had the joy of working together for several years, training church leaders around the world to prevent and correctly respond to sexual abuse. She is a skilled co-teacher who connects well with our students, sharing life-changing content with compassion and sensitivity. Her boldness in sharing her own story has helped many begin the healing journey by speaking up about their own hurts. I am so proud to be her co-worker!

It has been obvious in many of our conversations that Lisa's heart clearly aches for survivors, wanting them to know that God is the only source of true healing. Now you can join the conversation as you read *God is for Me*. Lisa draws us in by compassionately telling the stories of brave women of the Bible and clarifying the hurtful things they experienced that don't come up in Sunday School lessons. This refreshing honesty allows us to identify with them, realize we are not alone in the aftermath of our own horror stories, and maybe even help us feel heard. There are people who think that the Bible doesn't talk about abuse – which would mean at best that God doesn't care about survivors and at worst He condones abuse. We can sense Lisa's passion as she gets to the heart of her message, making it clear that the Bible certainly does address abuse, God condemns abuse of every type, and He longs to comfort survivors with His healing presence. It is beautiful to see her deftly digging deeply into God's Word to encounter His heart on various subjects related to abuse and healing from it. Finally, Lisa invites us to continue the conversation with God Himself, leaving us with references and questions that have no easy answers but that always lead us back to God's love. If you only have time to read one book other than the Bible, I strongly encourage that you choose this one!

Karen Shogren, founder of Levanta La Voz (Raise Your Voice)

God is for Me is an encouraging read for those who have experienced exploitation and abuse to deal and heal biblically. Lisa knows the heart of the reader as she transparently uses examples of women in scripture to offer support to the women of today. This book is an empowering source to bring wholeness for those struggling with the brokenness from sexual harm.

Verna Bowman, Precepts Bible Study leader, author of *Crumbs Along the Broken Path*

For too long, exegetes have regarded the women of the Bible as minor players at best; and, at worst, as sexual distractions to men's sanctity. Such interpretations are not rooted in Scripture, but cultural values that presume the heroes of the faith must be male.

God is for Me reveals, through close biblical reading, that God's daughters are not mere supporting actresses. Indeed, where women have been particularly vulnerable—especially to sexual predation—God is pleased to lead them to victory. I highly recommend what Lisa has achieved in this volume, in which she reintroduces us to women we thought we already knew and to the God who watches over them.

Gary S. Shogren, PhD, University of Aberdeen

To my fellow survivors that are bravely facing the painful wounds left by sexual abuse wondering if your God sees or cares, I have been where you are. Having more questions than answers and feeling as if God was absent from my heartbreaking reality. The healing journey we are on is a slow, little by little process. When you open this book, you will find words that bring both comfort and challenge. So, be patient with yourself as you read and take the time you need to process, find strength in the validation and wrestle with the parts that are hard. I pray for you my courageous sister or brother that as you walk the long road of healing ahead you that you will discover as I have the patient care of the Good Shepherd.

Anonymous Survivor

God is for Me

A Biblical Character Study of God's Heart for the Sexually Harmed

Lisa J. Radcliff

Copyright © 2026 by Lisa J. Radcliff

All rights reserved. No part of this publication may be reproduced, stored in a retrieval system, or transmitted in any form or by any means—electronic, mechanical, photocopying, recording, or otherwise—without prior written permission of the copyright holder, except for brief quotations used in reviews or scholarly works.

ISBN: 978-1-963377-60-6

Library of Congress Control Number: 2026931388

Abundance Books
Kalamazoo, Michigan

www.abundance-books.com

Printed in the United States of America

10 9 8 7 6 5 4 3 2 1

Cover design by Amber Weigand-Buckley, Barfaced Media

Unless otherwise noted, Scripture quotations are from THE HOLY BIBLE, ENGLISH STANDARD VERSION (ESV): Scriptures taken from THE HOLY BIBLE, ENGLISH STANDARD VERSION ® Copyright© 2001 by Crossway, a publishing ministry of Good News Publishers. Used by permission.

Scriptures marked NASB are taken from the NEW AMERICAN STANDARD (NAS): Scripture taken from the NEW AMERICAN STANDARD BIBLE®, copyright© 1960, 1962, 1963, 1968, 1971, 1972, 1973, 1975, 1977, 1995 by The Lockman Foundation. Used by permission.

Scriptures marked NIV are taken from the NEW INTERNATIONAL VERSION (NIV): Scripture taken from THE HOLY BIBLE, NEW INTERNATIONAL VERSION ®. Copyright© 1973, 1978, 1984, 2011 by Biblica, Inc.™. Used by permission of Zondervan

Dedication

To my sisters in the fight—those fighting
and those sharing their weapons,

God is for you!

Contents

Introduction — 15

Chapter One — 19
*God's Heart of Compassion:
Hagar's Story*

Chapter Two — 29
*God's Heart of Redemption:
Rahab's Story*

Chapter Three — 37
*God's Heart of Justice:
The Concubine's Story*

Chapter Four — 49
*God's Heart of Restoration:
Bathsheba's Story*

Chapter Five — 65
*God's Heart of Love:
Tamar's Story*

Chapter Six — 77
*God's Heart of Protection:
Esther's Story*

Chapter Seven   89
   God's Heart of Grace:
   The Samaritan Woman's Story

Chapter Eight   99
   God's Heart of Gentleness:
   The Adulterous Woman's Story

Chapter Nine   109
   God's Heart of Forgiveness:
   The Party Crasher's Story

Chapter Ten   119
   This I Know, That God Is for Me

Leader Notes   127

Bonus Chapter   135
   My Story

Acknowledgments   137

Introduction

A woman sits in the back of the church, fear welling inside her and threatening to burst out through tears. She struggles to hold it in. She doesn't want anyone to think she's any different from the rest of the congregation. If they knew her past, they would reject her.

It's happened before. More than once.

But as the pastor reaches the apex of his sermon—that God cares for the weak and vulnerable, and that those who harm them will be held accountable—the floodgates give way.

She's heard this before, and she wants to believe it. But when she shared her story of being abused as a child, her church's reaction did more harm. They asked what she had done, how she had gotten into that relationship, and why she was in that place at that time. Church members looked at her differently. They stopped talking to her or including her in their gatherings.

Intrusive thoughts accused her: *Could the abuse really have been her fault? Was there any hope for her? Would she ever be accepted? Could anyone really love her? Could God love her?*

This woman could be any of the women in your church, or it might be you. It reflects my experience when I first shared my story of sexual abuse with my church family. That was over thirty-five years ago. The church, in general, wasn't ready to hear about sexual abuse, certainly not on a Sunday morning. But my pastor urged me to share it as part of my testimony. I thought it was a bad idea. He thought the church needed to hear about this kind of abuse. It turned out we were both right. For many survivors today, this is still the reaction of their church family.

Look around at your congregation next time they gather for worship. Count off every fourth woman. At least that many have experienced sexual harm, usually before their eighteenth birthday. How many of them are barely holding it together on a Sunday morning? Even more importantly, how do we minister to them?

As Christians, we know the Bible is the inerrant Word of God. 2 Timothy 3:16 tells us that "all Scripture is breathed out by God and profitable for teaching, for reproof, for correction, and for training in righteousness." It's our trustworthy source for godly living. But does the Bible address issues of sexual harm? How should Christians and the church respond to victims and perpetrators? Does a victim have to forgive those who harmed them, and what would that forgiveness even look like? Are there examples we can turn to in God's Word?

The answer to that last question is yes, it requires deeper study. You won't find *sexual abuse, sexual harm,* or *perpetrator* in a concordance, but the narratives are all throughout the pages of Scripture. And as Scripture, these stories are profitable for teaching, reproof, correction, and training in righteousness.

In this book, we'll uncover God's heart for the sexually harmed through studying the stories of nine women in the Bible. There are more stories like theirs in the Bible, but these nine will allow you to see God's heart and then apply what you learn to other stories of sexual harm—including your own.

Recovering from sexual abuse and trauma was not something the Bible's authors, or even classic commentators such as John Calvin or Matthew Henry, included in their writings. In their defense, sexual-trauma language and understanding have only existed since the latter part of the twentieth century. Moreover, abuse is not usually the main focus of the passages, so a traditional teaching approach would not have included a discussion on sexual abuse. We will be looking at these passages and these women with their abuse in mind, without losing or minimizing the main points of the passages.

I pray that each of you reading this book will find God's heart—his love, compassion, restoration, justice, and more.

I love how Dane Ortlund describes God's heart in *Gentle and Lowly: The Heart of Christ for Sinners and Sufferers*, "When we speak of God's heart, we're speaking of the spring-loaded tilt of his affections, his natural bent, the regular flow of who he is and what he does . . . He isn't like you. Even the most intense of human love is but the faintest echo of heaven's cascading abundance. His heartful thoughts for you outstrip what you can conceive."[1]

Introduction

    I pray that you will understand, in your heart and your mind, that he is for you. I pray you will be open to the hard things that Scripture sometimes shows us, like how God uses man's evil for his glory. And I pray that you will be blessed by taking this journey into the heart of God.

> "God is too good to be unkind,
>
> too wise to be mistaken,
>
> and when we cannot trace his hand,
>
> we must trust his heart."
>
> Charles Spurgeon

Chapter One
God's Heart of Compassion:
Hagar – It's Not Your Fault

Hagar's Story
Genesis 16:1–12

Now Sarai, Abram's wife, had borne him no children. She had a female Egyptian servant whose name was Hagar. And Sarai said to Abram, "Behold now, the LORD has prevented me from bearing children. Go in to my servant; it may be that I shall obtain children by her." And Abram listened to the voice of Sarai. So, after Abram had lived ten years in the land of Canaan, Sarai, Abram's wife, took Hagar the Egyptian, her servant, and gave her to Abram her husband as a wife. And he went in to Hagar, and she conceived. And when she saw that she had conceived, she looked with contempt on her mistress. And Sarai said to Abram, "May the wrong done to me be on you! I gave my servant to your embrace, and when she saw that she had conceived, she looked on me with contempt. May the LORD judge between you and me!" But Abram said to Sarai, "Behold, your servant is in your power; do to her as you please." Then Sarai dealt harshly with her, and she fled from her.

The angel of the LORD found her by a spring of water in the wilderness, the spring on the way to Shur. And he said, "Hagar, servant of Sarai, where have you come from and where are you going?" She said, "I am fleeing from my mistress Sarai." The angel of the LORD said to her, "Return to your mistress and submit to her." The angel of the LORD also said to her, "I will surely multiply your offspring so that they cannot be numbered for multitude." And the angel of the LORD said to her,

"Behold, you are pregnant

and shall bear a son.

You shall call his name Ishmael,

because the LORD has listened to your affliction.

He shall be a wild donkey of a man,

his hand against everyone

and everyone's hand against him,

and he shall dwell over against all his kinsmen."

So she called the name of the Lord who spoke to her, "You are a God of seeing," for she said, "Truly here I have seen him who looks after me." Therefore the well was called Beer-lahai-roi; it lies between Kadesh and Bered.

And Hagar bore Abram a son, and Abram called the name of his son, whom Hagar bore, Ishmael. Abram was eighty-six years old when Hagar bore Ishmael to Abram.

Genesis 16:1–12

Who Was Hagar?

Hagar was an Egyptian woman who was a servant of Sarai. Abram was very wealthy and had large numbers of livestock as well as servants. When Sarai gave her to Abram as his "wife," her status was promoted from servant to concubine, which had certain rights attached to it under the Laws of Hammurabi, which was the law of the land at that time.[2]

God had made a covenant with Abram. He promised that Abram would have offspring in his old age. But Abram and Sarai had been in the land for ten years, and so far, no offspring. So Sarai took things into her own hands and gave Hagar to Abram as his wife to have a baby through her.

When God made the covenant with Abram, Abram believed God, and it was counted to him as righteousness (Genesis 15:6). Abram could have—and should have—told Sarai, "No, we must trust God. He will do what he promised." But he didn't. Sarai took Hagar and gave her to Abram, and he went in to her and she conceived.

It seems obvious what happened here. What we don't know is how Hagar felt about what happened. Sarai "took" her. This could be a figure of speech, or it could indicate Hagar was not a willing volunteer for this assignment. The same form of the word is used when Joseph's brothers "took" Joseph and threw him into the pit (Genesis 37:24 NASB1995). Perhaps Hagar volunteered to be a surrogate mother for Sarai. But the text doesn't say that, and the context doesn't suggest it, so it's more likely she was forced into a sexual relationship with Abram. Perhaps, in Hagar's culture this was expected of a servant. But, again, that doesn't tell us her feelings about it. It seems obvious that a woman involved in a sexual relationship that wasn't her choice suffered harm from it.

This method of childbearing may have been culturally acceptable, but it wasn't God's design. Abram and Sarai were to be set apart, following God and not the culture. Using a culturally acceptable method to meet their needs showed a lack of trust in their God.

The Abuse of Hagar

Did their actions rise to the level of abuse? Karen Shogren, founder of Levanta La Voz, a ministry that trains faith communities to confront sexual harm, defines abuse as "any type of non-accidental, ill-treatment, or neglect that causes harm or has the potential to harm which is done by someone in a position of responsibility, trust, or power over the victim."[3] So, any adult sexual relationship that is not consensual is abuse. I think we can say, therefore, that Hagar was sexually abused by Abram and Sarai. Abram sexually violated her, but Sarai was the one who forced her into it. We would say, in modern terminology, that Sarai trafficked Hagar. Sex trafficking is defined as "a type of exploitation where a person is forced to engage in sexual activities for the benefit of the exploiter."[4]

Sarai used this plan to benefit herself. She was the exploiter. Sarai and Abram had all the power. When it comes down to it, all abuse is an abuse of power. Someone with more power than another uses that power to harm them—that is the essence of abuse. Look at the power difference between Hagar and Sarai and Abram. Hagar had no husband to protect her. She was a foreigner. She was a woman. She was a servant. She was younger. Sarai and Abram held all the power. And they abused that power.

Once Hagar conceived, her demeanor toward Sarai changed. She viewed her with contempt. Was that due to what Sarai and Abram had done to her? Was it because she was pregnant and finally felt like she had some power that Sarai did not? Was she flaunting the fact that she could conceive? The Bible doesn't clarify that, but it does say that Sarai's demeanor toward Hagar changed as well.

Sarai started to mistreat her. She lowered her status to "slave." We don't know what the mistreatment was, but it was bad enough to force Hagar to run away. According to Mary York of Modern Reformation, "The semantic range of the word 'mistreat' in Hebrew includes and even leans toward force or physical violence, so when we read that Sarai mistreated Hagar, it is no small thing."[5]

If Hagar thought Abram would protect her, since she was carrying his child, she was wrong. He didn't offer her any protection. Instead, he told Sarai to do whatever she wanted with Hagar. He showed a serious lack of compassion for this woman whom he had used to suit his own purposes. Hagar probably felt like she had no one, no hope, and no choice but to run away. This is a story often repeated in today's society.

God's Heart Toward Hagar

With no plan and no way to care for herself or her child, Hagar took off. This is where we see God's heart for this abused woman with no hope. He found her by a spring of water in the wilderness. It's significant that he "found" her. It means that he sought her out—and that is what he does for each one of us. He pursues us. He seeks us. Joni Eareckson Tada puts it this way: "Our great king is eager to pour favor on his children. He does not wait for us to come to him; he seeks us out. He *actively* pursues us."[6] What we read here in Genesis 16 is a theophany: a physical appearing of God to man. It was not just any "angel of the LORD," but *the* "Angel of the LORD," a manifestation of God himself, seeking out one who was lost.

The offspring Hagar was carrying was not the promised one, not part of the covenant. Yet God didn't leave her alone in the wilderness with no hope. He went after her. And then he had a conversation with her. He didn't just order her back home or farther into the wilderness. He showed compassion by listening to her and really hearing her. And then, to further show how much he cared, he made promises to her concerning her baby. He promised to bless Ishmael and make him great, even knowing that his people would be enemies of God's promised people and cause them great strife. The Ishmaelites would not only be in constant conflict with them, but they would also cause God's people to reject him and follow after other gods.

Hagar was so moved by the compassion shown to her by the Angel of the Lord, she gave him a name: El-Roi, or "You are the God of Seeing." This hopeless, abused woman bestowed a new name on him because he "saw" her, really saw her. He saw her pain. He saw her hopelessness. He saw her need. He also saw her worth. God went to Hagar and showed her exactly who he is. And so she said, "Truly, I have seen him who looks after me."

God did what Abram and Sarai failed to do. They missed an opportunity to demonstrate their faith in their covenant God. They were a poor reflection of him. They didn't see Hagar as a person with worth, made in God's image. They only saw a way to get what they wanted by using her, rejecting God's promise. They should have been the ones looking after Hagar, protecting her. But where they failed, God didn't.

God's Grace Extends to Everyone

Abraham and Sarah (their names were changed by God in Genesis 17) are both listed in the Hall of Faith in Hebrews 11. How could these two make the list when they participated in such abuse? This is where we see God's grace extended to all of us, regardless of what we have done—a theme that will be repeated in this study. They were wrong to take advantage of Hagar, but this sinful act didn't define them, just like our sins don't define us.

Their faith would be tested again and again, and they would pass most of those tests. And when they didn't, they could start again with a clean slate. That's how God's forgiveness works. God doesn't keep an account of our wrongs. He removes them "as far as the east is from the west" (Psalm 103:12). It's as if they never happened.

That may be hard for an abuse victim to hear. Forgiveness is not for the innocent; it is for sinners. God's forgiveness is sufficient for any and every sinner, no matter how grievous the sin. When a sinner repents,

God sees them through the blood of his perfect Son, Jesus. It is grace upon grace, or none of us would be able to stand before him.

This doesn't mean that someone guilty of sexual abuse or misconduct should be allowed to continue in a leadership position or ministry position or not have to go to jail. Sin still has consequences. "As if their sin never happened" is that person's stance before God. Their guilt will require appropriate action at the human level.

Hagar Returns

God told Hagar to return to Sarai and submit to her. He didn't promise that her circumstances would change, he just directed her to return. What I believe changed is that Hagar no longer felt alone and without protection because she had met the "God of seeing" and "him who looks after me" (v. 13). What God was telling her to do was not the easy thing. He could have looked after her in the wilderness and wherever she was going, but that was not his plan for her. So Hagar returned to Sarai.

Hagar gave birth to Ishmael, and they lived under Abram and Sarai's authority for about the next fifteen years. The Bible doesn't tell us any more about the relationship between Hagar and Sarai during that time. Then thirteen years after Ishmael's birth, Sarah finally gave birth to Isaac, the son of the promise. The relationship between Sarah and Hagar was once again strained:

> And the child grew and was weaned. And Abraham made a great feast on the day that Isaac was weaned. But Sarah saw the son of Hagar the Egyptian, whom she had borne to Abraham, laughing. So she said to Abraham, "Cast out this slave woman with her son, for the son of this slave woman shall not be heir with my son Isaac." And the thing was very displeasing to Abraham on account of his son. But God said to Abraham, "Be not displeased because of the boy and because of your slave woman. Whatever Sarah says to you, do as she tells you, for through Isaac shall your offspring be named. And I will make a nation of the son of the slave woman also, because he is your offspring." So Abraham rose early in the morning and took bread and a skin of water and gave it to Hagar,

putting it on her shoulder, along with the child, and sent her away. And she departed and wandered in the wilderness of Beersheba.

When the water in the skin was gone, she put the child under one of the bushes. Then she went and sat down opposite him a good way off, about the distance of a bowshot, for she said, "Let me not look on the death of the child." And as she sat opposite him, she lifted up her voice and wept. And God heard the voice of the boy, and the angel of God called to Hagar from heaven and said to her, "What troubles you, Hagar? Fear not, for God has heard the voice of the boy where he is. Up! Lift up the boy, and hold him fast with your hand, for I will make him into a great nation." Then God opened her eyes, and she saw a well of water. And she went and filled the skin with water and gave the boy a drink. And God was with the boy, and he grew up. He lived in the wilderness and became an expert with the bow. He lived in the wilderness of Paran, and his mother took a wife for him from the land of Egypt.

Genesis 21:8–21

Sarah saw Ishmael laughing at a feast held for Isaac—and laughing was for Isaac (Sarah laughed when told she would bear a son in her old age, and Isaac's name means "he laughs"). Sarah's jealousy turned toward Ishmael, and there wasn't enough room in the family tent for both boys, as far as Sarah was concerned. She told Abraham to send them away. Abraham loved Ishmael, and it hurt him to force him to leave, but God told him to listen to the voice of Sarah. Ishmael was not the son of promise. So, Abraham gave Hagar some food and water and sent them away.

Once again, God found them in the wilderness, where Hagar was expecting they would die. But God stepped in, because he saw them, and showed her a well. This time, he didn't send her back. That season was over. Ishmael was becoming a man, so Hagar would have someone to take care of her. God had kept her safe and provided for her and would continue to keep his promises to her.

What is God's heart for Hagar?

Compassion – In Exodus 34:6 (NIV) God proclaims himself to be compassionate. Compassion results in action. In God's case it is in showing mercy, providing for a need, keeping his promises, and much more.

* How did God show compassion to Hagar and to Sarah?

* How does he show compassion to you?

* Are you surprised God sought out Hagar and made promises to her? Why or why not? (See also Romans 9:15.)

* Look at Matthew 9:36. In what ways did Jesus demonstrate compassion?

* Look at Psalm 103:13–14. God's compassion is as a loving father. What actions would you expect from a loving father?

How can we apply the lessons from Hagar's story?

It was not your fault

Hagar was a victim of sexual abuse. If her story were to appear on the news or on social media today, what questions do you think people would ask? Probably the first one would be, "What did she do to entice him into sleeping with her?" Others might be, "What was she wearing? . . . What was she doing near his tent? . . . What type of reputation does she have?"

Sadly, many survivors believe that the abuse they suffered was their fault. That can come from several sources—the abuser may have told the survivor it was her fault, the victim might not be believed, or the abuser might be revered by others, to name just a few. But abuse and other forms of sexual harm are *never* the fault of the victim, no matter what they were doing or wearing. Every survivor needs to know that what they suffered was not their fault.

All abuse is an abuse of power

* What were the power imbalances in this story?

* How did Abram and Sarai use their power and how should they have used their power?

* Where do you see abuses of power today?

* What can we (individually and as the church) do to help the vulnerable?

Victim blaming, or revictimizing, is wrong and causes further harm. Often when abuse is exposed, the victim of the abuse is blamed. We saw this in the case of Ravi Zacharias. After the first accusation of abuse, the leadership of his ministry (many were family members) circled the wagons and defamed the victim, revictimizing her and further abusing their power. Eventually, her case and others were found to be true.[7]

It took someone within the chain to break it, which is often the case. Someone has to say, "This is wrong. We can't treat people this way. This is abuse." And the victims must be given protection from further abuse. Sarai blamed Abram, saying, "God judge between you and me." God will judge sin, and the unrepentant will pay the price.

If you have experienced that sort of treatment, I'm truly sorry for what you've endured. It was wrong. Blaming the victim is unhelpful at best, and it can also lead to further abuse, emotional devastation, and destruction of the family/ministry/organization—not to mention a horrific misrepresentation of Christ/the church/Christianity.

It takes just one person to take a stand and say, "What happened was abuse and it was wrong." Call out the abuser and care for the victim. Whatever consequences come, even if it means the end of a ministry, the responsibility for that is solely on the shoulders of the abuser, not the victim. Judging those who do harm, and protecting the vulnerable is what God calls us to do:

> God has taken his place in the divine council;
>
> in the midst of the gods he holds judgment:
>
> "How long will you judge unjustly
>
> and show partiality to the wicked? Selah
>
> Give justice to the weak and the fatherless;

maintain the right of the afflicted and the destitute.

Rescue the weak and the needy;

deliver them from the hand of the wicked."

Psalm 82:1–4

If you are a survivor of abuse, God sees you and is for you.

If you have experienced harm at the hands of people you trusted in places you trusted, remember that God is El-Roi, the God Who Sees. He sees you, and he will have compassion on you. He also has a purpose for all you have suffered. Trust him. Remember Hagar and God's heart of compassion for her. It is for you too.

Chapter Two
God's Heart of Redemption:
Rahab – A Transformed Life

Rahab's Story

Joshua 2:1–21; 6:20-25

And Joshua the son of Nun sent two men secretly from Shittim as spies, saying, "Go, view the land, especially Jericho." And they went and came into the house of a prostitute whose name was Rahab and lodged there. And it was told to the king of Jericho, "Behold, men of Israel have come here tonight to search out the land." Then the king of Jericho sent to Rahab, saying, "Bring out the men who have come to you, who entered your house, for they have come to search out all the land." But the woman had taken the two men and hidden them. And she said, "True, the men came to me, but I did not know where they were from. And when the gate was about to be closed at dark, the men went out. I do not know where the men went. Pursue them quickly, for you will overtake them." But she had brought them up to the roof and hid them with the stalks of flax that she had laid in order on the roof. So the men pursued after them on the way to the Jordan as far as the fords. And the gate was shut as soon as the pursuers had gone out.

Before the men lay down, she came up to them on the roof and said to the men, "I know that the LORD has given you the land, and that the fear of you has fallen upon us, and that all the inhabitants of the land melt away before you. For we have heard how the LORD dried up the water of the Red Sea before you when you came out of Egypt, and what you did to the two kings of the Amorites who were beyond the Jordan, to Sihon and Og, whom you devoted to destruction. And as soon as we heard it, our hearts melted, and there was no spirit left in any man because of you, for the LORD your God, he is God in the heavens above and on the earth beneath. Now then, please swear to me by the LORD that, as I have dealt kindly with you, you also will deal kindly with my father's house, and give me a sure sign that you will save alive my father and mother, my brothers and sisters, and all who belong to them, and deliver our lives from death." And the men said to her, "Our life for yours even to death! If you do not tell this business of ours, then when the LORD gives us the land we will deal kindly and faithfully with you."

Then she let them down by a rope through the window, for her house was built into the city wall, so that she lived in the wall. And she said to them, "Go into the hills, or the pursuers will encounter you, and hide there three days until the pursuers have returned. Then afterward you may go your way." The men said to her, "We will be guiltless with respect to this oath of yours that you have made us swear. Behold, when we come into the land, you shall tie this scarlet cord in the window through which you let us down, and you shall gather into your house your father and mother, your brothers, and all your father's household. Then if anyone goes out of the doors of your house into the street, his blood shall be on his own head, and we shall be guiltless. But if a hand is laid on anyone who is with you in the house, his blood shall be on our head. But if you tell this business of ours, then we shall be guiltless with respect to your oath that you have made us swear." And she said, "According to your words, so be it." Then she sent them away, and they departed. And she tied the scarlet cord in the window.

Joshua 2:1–21

So the people shouted, and the trumpets were blown. As soon as the people heard the sound of the trumpet, the people shouted a great shout, and the wall fell down flat, so that the people went up into the city, every man straight before him, and they captured the city. Then they devoted all in the city to destruction, both men and women, young and old, oxen, sheep, and donkeys, with the edge of the sword.

But to the two men who had spied out the land, Joshua said, "Go into the prostitute's house and bring out from there the woman and all who belong to her, as you swore to her." So the young men who had been spies went in and brought out Rahab and her father and mother and brothers and all who belonged to her. And they brought all her relatives and put them outside the camp of Israel. And they burned the city with fire, and everything in it. Only the silver and gold, and the vessels of bronze and of iron, they put into the treasury of the house of the LORD. But Rahab the prostitute and her father's household and all who belonged to her, Joshua saved alive. And she has lived in Israel to this day, because she hid the messengers whom Joshua sent to spy out Jericho.

Joshua 6:20–25

Who Was Rahab?

Rahab is one of my favorite Bible characters because of the transformation God made in her, from prostitute to a woman in the Hall of Faith and a mother in the line of Jesus. Still, almost every time we read her name in Scripture, it is followed by the descriptor of her past—Rahab the harlot—lest we forget where she came from. But God used her to save his people and saved her in the process, which is great encouragement for anyone with an ugly past.

We first meet Rahab in Joshua 2. She was a prostitute in Jericho. Israel has just crossed the Jordan, and Jericho stood in their way to occupying the promised land. They had fought battles alongside God, "who performed many miracles and gave them victory." These things reached the ears of those living in Jericho, and according to Rahab, the hearts of the people melted in fear of them and their God.

Spies showed up at Rahab's house, and she took care of them, hiding them when city officials came looking for them. She told the spies that she wanted to follow their God, and because of her kindness to them, they promised to spare her life and the lives of any family members in her home. Rahab gathered all the family she could into her house, and all of them were saved. Her house was the only thing left standing in Jericho. Rahab and her family moved on with Israel. Though not Israelites, they had the protection and blessing that came with being part of Israel.

The good news of salvation is for everyone who believes (see Romans 1:16). What Rahab found out is that God's kindness leads to salvation. That kindness has not changed. It still draws sinners to salvation—those who have been harmed, those who harm others, and everyone in between.

God Redeems Our Stories

One of the amazing things God does is redeem our stories. We may have stories like Rahab's. Maybe we lived lives that were sinful and in deliberate disobedience to God. Or maybe our story is full of sinful acts done against us that have left us feeling hopeless. No matter which, God takes the things that happened to us and uses them for good (see Romans 8:28). Sometimes he uses them to bring us to our lowest place, where we see our need for him. Sometimes, like for Rahab, he miraculously removes us from our horrible circumstances and turns our lives around. As we walk with him, we continue to grow and learn, and at some point, we see how God worked in our lives to take us from darkness to light. From lives of slavery to sin to lives of freedom in Christ.

Rahab's life completely changed, from prostitute in Jericho to a sojourner with Israel. She was free from her past and able to begin again. And she did. Something about her drew the attention of an Israelite named Salmon. God blessed their marriage with a baby boy, Boaz.

Rahab: A Godly Mother

The story of Boaz is found in the book of Ruth. He is a man of integrity, compassion, and kindness. He is also called a kinsman redeemer, an example of the One who will redeem Israel. I can't help but believe he became that kind of man because of the love, instruction, and example of his mother. Ruth got Boaz's attention because of her character, specifically her love and care for her mother-in-law. Did that pull at his heartstrings, thinking of his own mother? I'm sure he knew her story, but it was probably unbelievable to him because of the woman he knew her to be.

Living among God's people, Rahab learned their ways and God's laws. She heard the blessings and curses shouted between the mountains, and she heard that they were for her too, the sojourner:

> And all Israel, sojourner as well as native born, with their elders and officers and their judges, stood on opposite sides of the ark before the Levitical priests who carried the ark of the covenant of the LORD, half of them in front of Mount Gerizim and half of them in front of Mount Ebal, just as Moses the servant of the LORD had commanded at the first, to bless the people of Israel. And afterward he read all the words of the law, the blessing and the curse, according to all that is written in the Book of the Law. There was not a word of all that Moses commanded that Joshua did not read before all the assembly of Israel, and the women, and the little ones, and the sojourners who live among them.
>
> Joshua 8:33–35

Rahab saw God work miraculously among them. I believe she followed God's command to "love the LORD your God with all your heart and with all your soul and with all your might. And these words that I command you today shall be on your heart. You shall teach them diligently to your children, and shall talk of them when you sit in your house, and when you walk by the way, and when you lie down, and when you rise" (yy 6:5–7). Boaz's character is most likely a direct result of Rahab's faith in God.

Rahab is one of only four women mentioned in Jesus's genealogy in Matthew 1. She is given a place of honor. And Hebrews 11 includes Rahab in the Hall of Faith. God redeemed her and her story. He turned the life of a prostitute into a meaningful, impactful life in the history of Israel. He had an incredible plan for her that she probably couldn't see from the window of her house on the wall surrounding Jericho. As that wall crumbled, it took her old life with it. In the next chapter of her life, she started out as an outcast but was soon brought into the family of God's chosen people. What a story!

Stepping Out of the Rubble

God still redeems stories. No matter our past, he has a plan for our good and his glory. It might require us to take scary steps to leave our past behind. Think about Rahab and her family in her house as the wall it was on came crashing down. Did she want to flee the house to get away, to try to save herself? She trusted the spies because they were God's people, and she knew what God had done for them already. Rahab remained in the place God had for her, with the red cord hanging out the window, letting the spies know where to find her after everything had collapsed.

Rahab stepped out of the rubble of her old life and into a completely new way of life. It must have been scary and confusing at times. That's how it is for those who have lived through abuse. Their world has been shattered. Even though it wasn't good, it was all they knew and leaving it is scary. They may have to leave behind people and places that were destructive but were also their source of life—income, home, friends, family, maybe even the ability to meet their basic needs.

Many abuse survivors feel like outcasts in their churches. They have been saved, but their past keeps them stuck, thinking God can't use them in his work. They don't seem to have a place in his church. Rahab's story shows us that God can and will use anyone who puts their faith in him, even if it is the size of a mustard seed (see Matthew 17:20). After all, it's not really Rahab's story or your story or my story; it's God's story.

What is God's heart for Rahab?

Redemption – God changes hearts and redeems people no matter their past (2 Corinthians 5:17; Colossians 3:3; Psalm 34:22).

* What does it mean to be redeemed? (See Ephesians 1:7; 1 Peter 1:18–19; Hebrews 9:15.)

* What has happened to your past? (See 2 Corinthians 5:17; Colossians 3:3; Psalm 34:22.)

* How should the redeemed now live? (See Galatians 2:20; 1 Corinthians 6:19-20; Romans 6:12-14.)

* If you haven't been redeemed—accepted that Jesus paid for your sins on the cross—what is keeping you from accepting God's free gift of salvation? (See Romans 6:23.)

Any story can be redeemed. Rahab is an excellent example of walking in newness of life. She left her old life behind, and became the mother of Boaz, a kinsmen redeemer (Ruth 2:1-12). Boaz was called a worthy man. He was full of integrity and honor, and it makes sense he was taught these virtues by his mother, Rahab. She taught her son God's ways.

* How has God redeemed your story?

* What difference has God's redemption made in your life?

How can we apply the lessons from Rahab's story?

Embrace a new life

Our broken places display God's glory (see 2 Corinthians 4:6-7). God can make your story of brokenness the place where his glory shines through you. Rahab's story is impactful because we know where she came from, what she was redeemed from. She was "Rahab the harlot," but became Rahab, mother of Boaz, a forerunner in the line of David and Jesus.

To embrace a new normal, we learn to walk in God's ways, teach them to our children (tell them our "stones of remembrance"), forget what lies behind, and press onward toward the prize (see Joshua 4:6-7). Telling our children, or the next generation, what the Lord has done for us—our story—will help them to remember his faithfulness. This story should always focus on what *God* did, *his* power, and the outcome or transformation he made in our lives (see Deuteronomy 10:12; Philippians 3:8-14).

* How can your story help others?
* How can your story glorify God?

If you feel like your past will always be part of your life, like Rahab the harlot, there is hope in the book of Revelation. Revelation 2:17 says that those who have trusted in Jesus for salvation will one day be given a new name. It will be written on a white stone—maybe like a stone of remembrance or maybe like one of those little reminder stones you keep in your pocket. Rahab will not eternally be known as the harlot. And you and I will have a new name given by Jesus. All things will become new, even our names.

* What are you most looking forward to about being made new?
* What does it mean to you to receive a new name?

Chapter Three

God's Heart of Justice:
The Levite's Concubine – Culture Shift

The Concubine's Story

Judges 19:1–4, 10–16, 20–30

It may be necessary to put a warning at the beginning of this chapter. It is the most violent story of sexual abuse in the Bible. Those who have experienced this type of trauma may be triggered by the narrative. Keep in mind our focus is on God's heart, and the concubine's story is a necessary one which points us to his justice.

> In those days, when there was no king in Israel, a certain Levite was sojourning in the remote parts of the hill country of Ephraim, who took to himself a concubine from Bethlehem in Judah. And his concubine was unfaithful to him, and she went away from him to her father's house at Bethlehem in Judah, and was there some four months. Then her husband arose and went after her, to speak kindly to her and bring her back. He had with him his servant and a couple of donkeys. And she brought him into her father's house. And when the girl's father saw him, he came with joy to meet him. And his father-in-law, the girl's father, made him stay, and he remained with him three days. So they ate and drank and spent the night there.
>
> [On the fifth night] . . . the man would not spend the night. He rose up and departed and arrived opposite Jebus (that is, Jerusalem). He had with him a couple of saddled donkeys, and his concubine was with him. When they were near Jebus, the day was nearly over, and the servant said to his master, "Come now, let us turn aside to this city of the Jebusites and spend the night in it." And his master said to him, "We will

not turn aside into the city of foreigners, who do not belong to the people of Israel, but we will pass on to Gibeah." And he said to his young man, "Come and let us draw near to one of these places and spend the night at Gibeah or at Ramah." So they passed on and went their way. And the sun went down on them near Gibeah, which belongs to Benjamin, and they turned aside there, to go in and spend the night at Gibeah. And he went in and sat down in the open square of the city, for no one took them into his house to spend the night.

And behold, an old man was coming from his work in the field at evening. The man was from the hill country of Ephraim, and he was sojourning in Gibeah. The men of the place were Benjaminites. . . . And the old man said, "Peace be to you; I will care for all your wants. Only, do not spend the night in the square." So he brought him into his house and gave the donkeys feed. And they washed their feet, and ate and drank.

As they were making their hearts merry, behold, the men of the city, worthless fellows, surrounded the house, beating on the door. And they said to the old man, the master of the house, "Bring out the man who came into your house, that we may know him." And the man, the master of the house, went out to them and said to them, "No, my brothers, do not act so wickedly; since this man has come into my house, do not do this vile thing. Behold, here are my virgin daughter and his concubine. Let me bring them out now. Violate them and do with them what seems good to you, but against this man do not do this outrageous thing." But the men would not listen to him. So the man seized his concubine and made her go out to them. And they knew her and abused her all night until the morning. And as the dawn began to break, they let her go. And as morning appeared, the woman came and fell down at the door of the man's house where her master was, until it was light.

And her master rose up in the morning, and when he

opened the doors of the house and went out to go on his way, behold, there was his concubine lying at the door of the house, with her hands on the threshold. He said to her, "Get up, let us be going." But there was no answer. Then he put her on the donkey, and the man rose up and went away to his home. And when he entered his house, he took a knife, and taking hold of his concubine he divided her, limb by limb, into twelve pieces, and sent her throughout all the territory of Israel. And all who saw it said, "Such a thing has never happened or been seen from the day that the people of Israel came up out of the land of Egypt until this day; consider it, take counsel, and speak."

Judges 19:1–4, 10–16, 20–30

A Bizarre Story

This story found in Judges 19 may be the least preached but most disturbing in all of Scripture. So many pastors skip chapter 19 as they preach through Judges, and it's no mystery why that is. Who would want to tackle the story of a woman who is thrown to sex-crazed men, is abused all night long, dies on the threshold of the home that should have been a safe place, and is then hacked to pieces, with one piece sent to each tribe of Israel?

The book of Judges is a historic narrative filled with amazing true stories. Skipping this one is understandable. It is not family-friendly—or the kind of story most people want to hear on a Sunday morning. But it is in the canon of Scripture, so therefore it is "profitable for teaching, for reproof, for correction, and for training in righteousness, that the man of God may be complete, equipped for every good work" (2 Timothy 3:16–17). In order to see the heart of God for the sexually harmed, we need to examine this story.

A bizarre account, it is also the most violent recount of sexual harm in the Bible, with the victim dying from the horrid severity of sexual violence she experienced. It could rival any current sexual violence story we see in the news today, and there is a lot we can learn from it, not just for application to personal stories but also for affecting the culture we live in.

This story took place within Israel, in a region belonging to the tribe of Benjamin. This is an important distinction. It might have been considered not so unusual outside of Israel, where pagan customs were the norm, but within Israel, where God's laws were clear regarding sexual behavior, it should have been unthinkable. Let's look first at the victim and the crime, and then we will address the culture.

Who Was This Woman?

A Levite and his concubine were traveling from her father's house, where she had run away after being unfaithful to her "husband" or master. It seems like it's going to be a loving story of forgiveness. The Levite "went after her, to speak kindly to her and bring her back" (v. 3). But then there was a strange sequence of leaving and staying another night, accompanied by a lot of eating and drinking. After five days of that, they finally hit the road.

The Levite also had a servant with him. Along their journey, the servant suggested they stop for the night in Jebus. This city would eventually become Jerusalem, but at the time it was occupied by the Jebusites, an Amorite tribe. The Benjaminites had infamously failed to drive the Amorites from the land when Israel took possession of what God had promised, and their disobedience led to exactly what God had warned them about: covenant people becoming like the evil people living among them.

Even though traveling at night was dangerous, the Levite decided to move on because, "We will not turn aside into the city of foreigners, who do not belong to the people of Israel. We will pass on to Gibeah" (paraphrase of v. 12). He understood the danger of spending the night among pagans, but he didn't realize their evil ways had permeated the people of Israel who were their neighbors.

They arrived in Gibeah, a city of Ephraim. The men living there were Benjaminites, and their first encounter was a good one, exactly what the Levite expected. An old man met them in the town square and offered them a place to stay. The Levite's decision seemed to have been a wise one. Their night started out perfectly, until it took a twist they didn't expect.

The men of the city came to the old man's home and insisted he give them the Levite so they could "know" him. This wasn't a "get to know him," as if they wanted to make a new friend; this was "know" in the sexual context. And things went from bad to worse. The old man suggested an alternative: "No, my brothers, do not act so wickedly; since this man has come into my house. Do not do this vile thing. Behold, here are my virgin daughter and his concubine. Let me bring them out now. Violate them and do what seems good to you, but against this man do not do this outrageous thing" (v. 23–24).

It seems that even this nice old man had been influenced by the culture around him. How could he have offered his own daughter, as well as the man's concubine, to be violated? Why didn't he protect *them* with as much vigilance as he was protecting the Levite? At the time, women were considered property. They didn't have the same standing as men. They didn't have the personhood that a man, especially a Levite, did in that culture. (Personhood is something that sexual violence still takes from its victims today.) But still, how could two men even think of putting women in this position?

The Deadly Violence of Sexual Assault

Now we come to the sexual assault that is so violent, it's hard to believe it's in the Bible. The fact that it's in there shows us that God cares about this issue and wants us to learn from it. But we must remember that it isn't just a story for us to learn from. It was an actual event that really happened to someone. There was a horrific crime and a victim.

That, too, can be hard to comprehend, but it is also wonderfully comforting. Psalm 33:11 (NIV) tells us, "But the plans of the LORD stand firm forever, the purposes of his heart through all generations." No matter what, no matter our circumstances or how evil the world around us is, he is there, and he has a plan for our good and his glory.

The man forced his concubine out the door and into the clutches of evil men who only wanted to satisfy their own sexual desires. That satisfaction was not going to be in a romantic, loving sexual way, but the most vile, violent way possible. The woman was gang raped—violently, repeatedly, all night long. As the sun rose, they finished with her, the light driving away the darkness. They let her go, and she stumbled back to the threshold of the old man's house where she collapsed and died.

A Corrupted Culture

The Levite opened the door and found her there. In a most unconcerned, unloving way, he told her, "Get up, let's go" (paraphrase of v.

28). But there was no answer. He picked her up and threw her on the donkey and set out for home. "When he reached home, he took a knife and cut up his concubine limb by limb, into twelve parts, and sent them into all the areas of Israel" (paraphrase of v. 29).

He did what? Why?

This is the culture part of this story. The Levite thought he was safe because he was within Israel's borders. He passed by the city he considered dangerous; the people of that city didn't have God's law or follow his law. He viewed the law as a safety net. What evil could happen to him in a city of God's law-following people?

The people of the next city weren't following God's law either, though. They had become like the culture around them. People who followed evil, pagan ways of life were living among them, influencing the Jewish people and Jewish culture. Instead of remembering how God had delivered their forefathers and being beacons of God's holiness, they turned from him to follow other gods and the sinful lifestyles of their followers. The ugliness that happened that night in Gibeah probably started years before with small compromises of faith. Over time, the people's hearts were far from God and fixed wholly on their own sinful desires.

In most cases, those who sexually harm others have much the same story, especially those who are involved in a church. They know what sin is and have been warned not to give in to temptation. But their own desires, often fueled by the culture around them—the things they watch online, on TV, on their phone, or hear on the radio begin to outweigh their desire to please God and follow him. The more they sin, the easier it gets and the more evil it gets. Eventually, someone who once identified as a God-follower is no different in their behavior from a pagan or a person who cares only about meeting their own desires, regardless of the harm they may cause to someone else.

The Levite sent pieces of his concubine throughout Israel to vividly show them how far from God they had gone. What was once was—and should have been—considered outrageous, unthinkable, and un-Jewish was happening within Israel. This had the desired effect: "And all who saw it said, 'Such a thing has never happened or been seen from the day that the people of Israel came up out of the land of Egypt until this day; consider it, take counsel, and speak'" (v. 30).

A Culture Shift

This shocking story knocked some sense into Israel. They did take counsel together, and they asked God what to do. That was a significant development. This was a time in Israel's history when there was no judge in Israel, and "everyone did what was right in his own eyes" (Judges 21:25). They had forsaken God's culture and developed their own. Anytime that happens, evil is sure to spread its tentacles far and wide until what was once unthinkable becomes normal. It may start small with minor infractions, every now and then doing something completely out of character. But little by little, that great evil doesn't seem so evil, and finally a culture accepts evil as normal.

Israel gathered together fighting men from each tribe, asked God what to do, and punished the tribe of Benjamin for their sin. The Levite's actions following the death of his concubine brought the sin to light in a way that couldn't be ignored.

For those who say God doesn't care about women or those sexually harmed, think about God's consequences for what happened to this woman. God's judgment on the rape and death of one woman was the deaths of more than 65,000 of Israel's fighting men. The tribes of Israel came together to fight against the tribe of Benjamin. They sought the Lord in prayer and fasting, and God kept telling them to go up against Benjamin, even though they suffered great losses in the first two campaigns. Clearly, he executed judgment. He took it very seriously. He didn't ignore it. He didn't allow it to be swept under the rug, and he used it to draw Israel back to himself. He cared about the concubine. His heart was for her, even though tragic circumstances were part of her story.

As God's people today, we need to do the same thing when we hear of sexual sin in our midst. Too often, the church has covered up sexual sin committed by church members or church leaders. How can we expect to positively affect the culture around us when we turn a blind eye to the culture within us?

Every church has a culture. It starts with leadership and filters down through the members, whose own experiences inform their beliefs. There are warning signs when a church culture has turned away from God's standard. Is the leadership secretive or transparent? Are members disappearing or is attendance dwindling with no explanation? Does leadership welcome discussion of problems or shoot down concerns? Are the leaders friends and relatives of one another? (Nepotism in the church can lay the groundwork for secrecy and protecting abusers.)

The authors of *A Church Called Tov: Forming a Goodness Culture that Resists Abuses and Promotes Healing* write, "The bad news and the good news about culture can be summed up in the same statement: A rooted culture is almost *irresistible*. If the reinforcing culture is toxic, it becomes systemically corrupted and corrupts the people within it. Like racism, sexism, political ideologies, and success-at-all-costs businesses, a corrupted culture drags everyone down with it. On the other hand, if the reinforcing culture is *redemptive* and *healing* and *good (tov)*, it becomes systemically good. A *tov* church culture will instinctively heal, redeem, and restore."[8]

Be The Church

In contrast, every sin doesn't need to be broadcast from the pulpit. How many of us would show up for Sunday services if our sins were going to be read aloud to the congregation? Church leaders walk a fine line sometimes. The kinds of sins that need to be made public are the ones that affect the whole body of believers. That can include a disclosure of sexual abuse within the church, sexual harm done by someone in leadership, or allegations of sexual abuse.

Why make allegations public knowledge? Because perpetrators of sexual abuse rarely have only one victim, and most victims remain silent until others come forward. Making a public announcement (without sharing the victim's name) may encourage other victims to come forward, which could be a first step in healing for them. That is my story. I never would have disclosed my abuse if someone else hadn't come forward first. It could also encourage the church to be the church, and weep with those who weep, pray for one another, and love the families affected in practical ways. It could be a circling of the wagons in a positive way, as the pioneers literally did to protect the most vulnerable among them.

What can we know of God's heart in this situation? He isn't mentioned at all in the story until the despicable act comes to light and Israel consults him. At that point, we see that he requires justice for this woman. According to Jewish law, the woman should have been stoned to death for being unfaithful. But even if that was what God required for her sin, sexual violence was not part of his justice.

The men of Gibeah weren't knocking on the old man's door to seek God's justice. They were there seeking gratification of their sinful desires. God's righteous judgment never entered their thinking. We don't know if the concubine was an Israelite or a God-follower. We know nothing about her except this one story, which is not her whole story. If she was one of God's people, we know her death was precious to him (see Psalm 116:15). If she was not one of his own, we know he did not delight in her death (see Ezekiel 33:11).

Suffering Has Purpose

God doesn't waste suffering. Whatever his reasons, this woman was to live out this story with a tragic end to her life for a purpose. Her brutal death and subsequent revealing of the sin within Israel caused a cultural shift. Unfortunately, that's often what it takes to make, or at least start, cultural change. Her story is still being told and still being used to bring awareness and affect change in how the church should view sexual sin, especially within its own borders.

Because God is sovereign, there is no such thing as an "untimely death." The death of a young person or a healthy older person might be unexpected, but it wasn't one moment sooner than God planned for it to be. If we really believe that the length of our days has already been determined by God (see Psalm 139:16), then there is no lost potential. That person has completed all that God determined for them to do. Not a single thread of the tapestry God was weaving of their life was left unwoven. The child with "so many years ahead of them" and the young pastor with "unfinished ministry" completed their races. Their finish line came quicker than expected, but there were no more races left to run. The concubine of Judges 19 met a tragic death, but it came about in God's perfect timing. There was nothing in life left for her to do, yet her story lives on to inform us.

When we allow survivors of abuse and sexual harm to share their stories in our churches, we keep the message of the Judges 19 concubine alive. The most tragic part of her story is that she was harmed so severely that she didn't survive. But her story did, and it should encourage other victims to share their stories and keep bringing the darkness into the light. Sharing their stories will help them heal and encourage other survivors to share their own stories and find healing.

And the church should support those survivors by giving them a platform for sharing their stories, providing resources for healing, loving them, and preaching passages like Judges 19.

What is God's heart for the Levite's Concubine?

Justice – In this passage, sexual sin is called wicked, unspeakable, outrageous, vile, evil, violating, and an abomination. How did Israel's culture get to this point? How did God show justice and mercy? (See Judges 20:24–28, 35.)

* Justice is in God's hands. Have you felt like you want to be the one to execute justice? How can you leave it with God even when it seems like he's not doing anything? (See Romans 12:19; Psalm 50:16–22.)

* Sometimes survivors get bound up in wanting justice so much that they live as if they are still prisoners to what happened to them (or to their own sin). Do you believe that God has set you free and that you can trust him for justice? (See Psalm 146:5–9; Psalm 56:7; Psalm 1:5–6.)

* God will not allow the wicked to go unpunished forever. Can you rest in knowing that God's justice will ultimately come to all who cause harm and do not repent? (See Revelation 19:11–12; 2 Thessalonians 1:6–7.)

How can we apply the lessons from the Concubine's story?

Culture Shift

Culture shifts can be caused by advances in science or medicine or other positive means. But culture also shifts as we become accustomed to sin and make it "normal."

* What shifts have you seen in the culture regarding sexuality and especially sexual harm?

* Has God changed in his judgment of sexual sin? (See 2 Peter 2:6–10, 14.)

* How can we shift the culture to see sexual sin as wicked?

* How should we as the church respond when we learn of sexual harm in our communities or congregations?

* Once evil is exposed, then what?

Part of creating a new normal in our culture is making sure we are doing everything we can to prevent abuse from happening. That includes creating protection policies in our churches and other places that have programs for children. There are key elements to policies, but the most important is that everyone understands and uses the policy. It does no good to have policies that are buried in a file. They should be reviewed and updated every year, along with yearly training (at least) for all staff and children's ministry volunteers.

Be The Church

We need to care for the survivors of evil. When perpetrators are husbands and fathers and go to jail or lose their job, what does their family need? How can the church be the church to those families? They may need financial support, playdates, legal help, or counseling. Ask them how you can help or offer your specific area of expertise. The family may be too embarrassed to ask for help, so offer without being asked.

If you are the survivor or in the family of a survivor, don't pull away from the church. Rather, lean into it. They are your spiritual body; they will hurt when you hurt and rejoice when you rejoice. But they won't automatically know what you need or when you're hurting or how to help. Let them into your pain and lean on their strength (see Galatians 6:2). Satan is all too happy to destroy Christian families. You need to remain connected to your church family. Of course, this is assuming you are in a healthy church. If abuse is happening within the church, or your church is not supportive in your healing process, find safe people and a safe place to heal.

Chapter Four
God's Heart of Restoration:
Bathsheba – Breaking the Silence

Bathsheba's Story

2 Samuel 11:1–27

In the spring of the year, the time when kings go out to battle, David sent Joab, and his servants with him, and all Israel. And they ravaged the Ammonites and besieged Rabbah. But David remained at Jerusalem.

It happened, late one afternoon, when David arose from his couch and was walking on the roof of the king's house, that he saw from the roof a woman bathing; and the woman was very beautiful. And David sent and inquired about the woman. And one said, "Is not this Bathsheba, the daughter of Eliam, the wife of Uriah the Hittite?" So David sent messengers and took her, and she came to him, and he lay with her. (Now she had been purifying herself from her uncleanness.) Then she returned to her house. And the woman conceived, and she sent and told David, "I am pregnant."

So David sent word to Joab, "Send me Uriah the Hittite." And Joab sent Uriah to David. When Uriah came to him, David asked how Joab was doing and how the people were doing and how the war was going. Then David said to Uriah, "Go down to your house and wash your feet." And Uriah went out of the king's house, and there followed him a present from the king. But Uriah slept at the door of the king's house with all the servants of his lord, and did not go down to his house. When they told David, "Uriah did not go down to his house," David said to Uriah, "Have you not come from a journey? Why did you not go down to your house?" Uriah said to David, "The ark and Israel and Judah dwell in booths, and my lord Joab and the servants of my lord are camping in the open field. Shall I then go to my house, to eat and to drink and to lie with my wife? As you live, and as your soul lives, I will not do this thing." Then David said to Uriah, "Remain here today also, and tomorrow I will send you back." So Uriah remained in Jerusalem that day and the next. And David invited him, and he ate in his presence and drank, so that he made him drunk. And in the evening he went out to lie on his couch with the servants of his lord, but he did not go down to his house.

In the morning David wrote a letter to Joab and sent it by the hand of Uriah. In the letter he wrote, "Set Uriah in the forefront of the hardest fighting, and then draw back from him, that he may be struck down, and die." And as Joab was besieging the city, he assigned Uriah to the place where he knew there were valiant men. And the men of the city came out and fought with Joab, and some of the servants of David among the people fell. Uriah the Hittite also died. Then Joab sent and told David all the news about the fighting. And he instructed the messenger, "When you have finished telling all the news about the fighting to the king, then, if the king's anger rises, and if he says to you, 'Why did you go so near the city to fight? Did you not know that they would shoot from the wall? Who killed Abimelech the son of Jerubbesheth? Did not a woman cast an upper millstone on him from the wall, so that he died at Thebez? Why did you go so near the wall?' then you shall say, 'Your servant Uriah the Hittite is dead also.'"

So the messenger went and came and told David all that Joab had sent him to tell. The messenger said to David, "The men gained an advantage over us and came out against us in the field, but we drove them back to the entrance of the gate. Then the archers shot at your servants from the wall. Some of the king's servants are dead, and your servant Uriah the Hittite is dead also." David said to the messenger, "Thus shall you say to Joab, 'Do not let this matter displease you, for the sword devours now one and now another. Strengthen your attack against the city and overthrow it.' And encourage him."

When the wife of Uriah heard that Uriah her husband was dead, she lamented over her husband. And when the mourning was over, David sent and brought her to his house, and she became his wife and bore him a son. But the thing that David had done displeased the LORD.

2 Samuel 11:1–27

Who Is Bathsheba?

The story of David and Bathsheba is very well-known, maybe too well-known. Is it so familiar that we don't know what the Bible really says? The way it has been traditionally taught is that it's a story of two adulterers, equally complicit in their sexual relationship. Some have even taught that Bathsheba was at fault for wanting and pursuing a sexual relationship with David. A painting by Jean Bourdichon (1457–1521) depicts a nude, seductive Bathsheba[9] outside David's window. But that is not what the Bible tells us. Could it be that Bathsheba was not an adulterer but a victim of sexual harm? You've already guessed my opinion, since she's the subject of a chapter in this book. Maybe we should take a look at the familiar story with fresh eyes and an open mind.

We read in 2 Samuel 11 that David was out on his roof, looking over his kingdom, during a time of year when he should have been with his army, fighting his enemies. The text doesn't tell us why he wasn't with them, or why he stayed at home. Maybe he had the sniffles and went out onto his roof for some fresh air. Maybe his motive for being there wasn't that he was looking for a woman. After all, he had wives—lots of them. If he had sex in mind, he didn't need to be outside. But that's where he was.

Enter Bathsheba, bathing. We don't know how close her house was to David's house, but close enough that he could see her. We don't know if she knew he could see her or was even looking in her direction. We don't even know if she was naked or using a basin while partially clothed. What we can be fairly confident of is that she wasn't bathing with the intent to attract a man. She was already married to a fine man—as we will find out soon enough.

Bathsheba was bathing to comply with Jewish law. Verse 4 tells us that she "had been purifying herself from her uncleanness." So the Bible is clear about the motive behind her bathing—the cleansing a woman was required to do after the bleeding from her menstrual cycle had ended. That's what she was doing when David saw her bathing. Every woman who has ever bled knows how great that bath or shower feels. Knowing how inconvenient the whole bleeding thing is today, imagine what it was like for women in Bathsheba's time. I bet she wasn't thinking of anything except how clean she felt.

A Snowball of Sin

Only one verse, verse 4, tells us what happened. David saw Bathsheba bathing and noticed that she was beautiful. While she was following God's law in purification, David's looking led him to break God's law in coveting another man's wife. And then things went from bad to worse. He sent messengers to her, took her, and lay with her. That does not sound like anything romantic. It doesn't sound like Bathsheba had any part in it other than being the object of David's desire.

What we see is one man's sin, multiplying quickly. First, he saw a woman, not his wife. Seeing her was not sin. He should have turned away and gone back into his house. But he didn't. He inquired about her and found out who she was. He still could have stopped there because he found out she was married to Uriah, one of his best soldiers. But he didn't stop. He coveted Uriah's wife. Finally, he "took" her and lay with her. That infers coercive sex, not consensual sex.

Of course, having sex during that stage of a woman's menstrual cycle is where babies come from, and yes, they knew that back then. Bathsheba got pregnant and sent word to David. And nothing changed: sin begot more sin. He tried to cover up that the baby was his by having Uriah come home from battle. But in this instance, Uriah was much more honorable than his king and wouldn't sleep with his wife while his fellow soldiers were at war. So, David had Uriah killed in battle. This whole sequence of sin started with whatever motivated David to stay home and look at a beautiful woman. Then it snowballed to lust, covetousness, abuse, and murder.

There is plenty of disagreement on what to call what happened between David and Bathsheba. But many of today's Bible scholars have moved away from the traditional co-complicit understanding of it to some form of sexual misconduct squarely falling on David's shoulders. Some do call it rape. If Bathsheba was coerced to have sex with David, we would certainly call that rape today. The problem is, the Bible doesn't use the word rape in this story. But, then again, the absence of the word doesn't mean it doesn't apply. We have to examine the context to find the truth when the words aren't completely clear.

The Bible does use the word *rape* in other stories (primarily in the NIV). It may indicate what happened to Bathsheba was not as violent as the stories where the word *rape* is used, as in the stories of Dinah (Genesis 34:2), the Levite's concubine (Judges 19), and Tamar (2 Samuel 13:14). Some argue that it was only rape if she cried out, citing Deuteronomy 22. But the Bible doesn't say the women mentioned above cried out, yet their stories are called rape.

Dr. David T. Lamb, Professor of Old Testament at Missio Seminary, writes:

> David took all the initiative to instigate the affair. He saw her, he inquired about her, he sent messengers to get her, he took her, and he laid with her. The only thing she did was agree to come when ordered by her sovereign. She would have no reason to suspect something sexual was afoot but probably thought David was going to give her news, most likely bad news, about the fate of her husband, Uriah, which is exactly what happens later in the story after David has him killed.[10]

He goes on to say, "If what happened between David and Bathsheba was adultery, then Bathsheba also deserved death, and the text should make that clear, as it does for David. Since the text places all of the blame on David and states that only he deserves death, based on Deuteronomy 22, we should assume that what took place was rape."[11]

All abuse is an abuse of power. When one party has more power than the other, abuse can take place. Did Bathsheba have the ability to say no to David? No. He was the king. What would have been the outcome for her? His position as king made it nearly impossible for her to do anything but allow him to do what he desired, regardless of how she felt about it. That is abuse. At the very least, David sexually abused Bathsheba because of how he used his power.

Confront the Perpetrator

David then dragged other people into his sin. The messengers who took Bathsheba surely knew the king wasn't inviting her for lunch. And Joab, his commander, was given a message from David with written instructions on how to make sure Uriah was killed in battle. Ironically, Uriah was the one delivering the message. David knew Uriah was so trustworthy he wouldn't look at the message before delivering it. Why did these men keep quiet, knowing that David's sin had spiraled down to murder? Did they fear for their own lives if they spoke up against the king? They saw what happened to Uriah, and he hadn't done anything against the king. They lacked the courage to confront sin in their king, but the prophet Nathan did not.

2 Samuel 12:1–24

> And the LORD sent Nathan to David. He came to him and said to him, "There were two men in a certain city, the one rich and the other poor. The rich man had very many flocks and herds, but the poor man had nothing but one little ewe lamb, which he had bought. And he brought it up, and it grew up with him and with his children. It used to eat of his morsel and drink from his cup and lie in his arms, and it was like a daughter to him. Now there came a traveler to the rich man, and he was unwilling to take one of his own flock or herd to prepare for the guest who had come to him, but he took the poor man's lamb and prepared it for the man who had come to him." Then David's anger was greatly kindled against the man, and he said to Nathan, "As the LORD lives,

the man who has done this deserves to die, and he shall restore the lamb fourfold, because he did this thing, and because he had no pity."

Nathan said to David, "You are the man! Thus says the LORD, the God of Israel, 'I anointed you king over Israel, and I delivered you out of the hand of Saul. And I gave you your master's house and your master's wives into your arms and gave you the house of Israel and of Judah. And if this were too little, I would add to you as much more. Why have you despised the word of the LORD, to do what is evil in his sight? You have struck down Uriah the Hittite with the sword and have taken his wife to be your wife and have killed him with the sword of the Ammonites. Now therefore the sword shall never depart from your house, because you have despised me and have taken the wife of Uriah the Hittite to be your wife.' Thus says the LORD, 'Behold, I will raise up evil against you out of your own house. And I will take your wives before your eyes and give them to your neighbor, and he shall lie with your wives in the sight of this sun. For you did it secretly, but I will do this thing before all Israel and before the sun.'" David said to Nathan, "I have sinned against the LORD." And Nathan said to David, "The LORD also has put away your sin; you shall not die. Nevertheless, because by this deed you have utterly scorned the LORD, the child who is born to you shall die." Then Nathan went to his house.

And the LORD afflicted the child that Uriah's wife bore to David, and he became sick. David therefore sought God on behalf of the child. And David fasted and went in and lay all night on the ground. And the elders of his house stood beside him, to raise him from the ground, but he would not, nor did he eat food with them. On the seventh day the child died. And the servants of David were afraid to tell him that the child was dead, for they said, "Behold, while the child was yet alive, we spoke to him, and he did not listen to us. How then can we say to him the child is dead? He may do himself some harm." But when David saw that his servants were whispering together, David understood that the child was dead. And David said to his servants, "Is the child dead?" They said, "He is dead." Then David arose from the earth and washed and anointed himself and changed his clothes. And he went into the house of the LORD and worshiped. He then went to his own house. And when he asked, they set food before him, and he ate. Then his servants said to him, "What is this thing that you have done? You fasted and wept for the child while he was alive; but when the child died, you arose and ate food." He said, "While the child was still alive, I fasted and wept, for I said, 'Who knows whether the LORD will be gracious to me, that the child may live?' But now he is dead. Why should I fast? Can I bring him back again? I shall go to him, but he will not return to me."

Then David comforted his wife, Bathsheba, and went in to her and lay with her, and she bore a son, and he called his name Solomon. And the LORD loved him.

2 Samuel 12:1–24

The Truth Exposed

Nathan confronted David with his sin by telling him a story that reveals the truth of David and Bathsheba. The story he told David of a rich man stealing a beloved ewe lamb from a poor man lays the responsibility completely on the rich man, who is David. The poor man represents Uriah, the one who loved his little lamb, his one and only lamb. That lamb is Bathsheba. In this illustration, the lamb is only portrayed as a victim, stolen and killed by the rich man with no regard for the lamb or the poor man.

And it's not just Nathan who solely blamed David. God never called Bathsheba an adulterer or said that she sinned. But in 2 Samuel 11:27, we find that after Bathsheba's time of mourning over Uriah was done, David took her as his wife, and she bore him a son. "But the thing that

David had done displeased the Lord." It doesn't say David and Bathsheba's sin displeased the Lord. It says David's sin displeased the Lord. Bathsheba was never condemned either by God or by Nathan. David himself recognized the lamb had no responsibility for what happened when he said in 2 Samuel 12:5-6 that the man deserved to die, and he shall restore the lamb fourfold. He was furious with this rich man.

Nathan had David just where he wanted him. At that point he hit him right between the eyes, as if he were Goliath: "You are the man!" Ouch. There are things at this point in the story that make me wonder. Was Bathsheba present for this storytelling? Did she know David had Uriah killed, or did she think (up until that moment) that he died in battle, just a casualty of war? Did she and David have a conversation about it? What was that like, especially after Nathan said God had removed the sin from David, but as a consequence the baby would die?

Another thing I wonder about is what David would have done if someone had pointed out his sin before it got to the point of taking Bathsheba to satisfy his lust. In the world of sexual abuse, it only takes one person saying, "This is wrong," to save a victim. What if one of his men had confronted him before it was too late? There was the person who revealed Bathsheba's identity to him. There were soldiers who went to get her. Surely, there were a number of people who understood what he was planning and could have stepped in to stop him. Maybe not, considering who he was. This was a clear abuse of power, and perhaps those around him were too afraid he would abuse his power toward them if they interfered.

The Suffering and Restoration of Bathsheba

Regardless of how the baby came to be, he was Bathsheba's child too. Not only did she endure sexual harm and the death of her husband, but now her baby was going to die. Her grief was all because of David's sin. This woman's suffering was great—greater than most of us will experience. But God's heart for her was restoration. During Nathan's story, David proclaimed that the lost lamb should be restored fourfold.

Bathsheba was restored, in part, by becoming David's wife. He could have banished her or put her away secretly. He was king. He could do whatever he wanted. But he didn't. He married Bathsheba. Even if he did it to preserve the illusion that their child wasn't the result of his sin, God used it as a means of restoration for Bathsheba.

It might not have been her preferred choice, but being the wife of the king had plenty of positive outcomes. She and her child would be cared for, provided for, and protected. Every need would be met; they would want for nothing. And, of course, she would have a relationship with David that was closer than most of his subjects.

When we talk about David, especially in light of this story, we may be tempted to only remember his faults. But David was the greatest king Israel ever knew. He was a man after God's own heart. God himself said that David followed him with his whole heart. He was an accomplished musician and songwriter. He worshiped and praised God with great joy. This was the man Bathsheba was married to.

Generations of kings to follow would be compared to him. The Bible judged future kings with phrases like, "He followed God as his father David had done." Or, "He didn't follow God wholly, as his father David had done." (See examples in 2 Kings 18:3; 16:2–4.)

There were myriad qualities in David to make being married to him pretty positive. Perhaps the greatest is his heart revealed in Psalm 51, his Psalm of repentance for the sin he committed in this very story. He truly wanted a clean heart and restored joy. I think God granted his request, and Bathsheba must have benefited from David's relationship with God as well.

While it may seem strange to us, in the account of the death of their son, David comforted Bathsheba and got her pregnant again. The timing of the comfort and the pregnancy isn't exactly clear, but they seem to at least be close together. David had promised Bathsheba that another of her sons would be David's successor as king of Israel. That son was Solomon. He wasn't even close to being next in line to the throne, but it was a promise made to Bathsheba. When it looked like Solomon's ascension to the throne was in jeopardy, Bathsheba and Nathan went to David, who kept his promise and immediately declared Soloman king. Again, Bathsheba's position is secured. Nathan also said that this move would save her life and the life of her son, another way we see God's heart of restoration.

Bathsheba is mentioned in the lineage of Jesus. Matthew calls her "the wife of Uriah," a reminder of her suffering and restoration. There are only four women mentioned in his lineage: Tamar (Judah's daughter-in-law), Rahab, Ruth, and Bathsheba. Three were involved in sexual harm in some way, and Ruth was a young widow and an outsider. I think Matthew 1 tells us a lot about God's heart for these women and what they suffered. This was a patriarchal society. That any women are mentioned is remarkable. He exalts them because he is a God of compassion and restoration.

The Restoration of David

Sometimes when we think of David's sin against Bathsheba and Uriah, we wonder how God could call him "a man after God's own heart." This is the ultimate restoration. God sees David without seeing his sin because David repented of his sin. Psalm 51 is his song of repentance, specifically derived from this story. David was truly repentant (vv. 1–4). He acknowledged his sin and lamented over it. He knew he deserved death. And he knew his son was going to die instead. He fasted and prayed in anguish that God would let his son live, but that is not what God did.

There were severe consequences for David's sin. But once the child died, David had his answer, and he was ready to go on. David needed a redeemer, someone who could restore his joy, and he found that in a merciful God. It was David himself who wrote, "As far as the east is from the west, so far does he remove our transgressions from us" (Psalm 103:12).

Repentance and forgiveness do not eliminate the consequences of sin. Sexual abuse, rape, and other forms of sexual harm are crimes and should be treated as such. As the church, we can't hide behind the grace of God, ignoring the civil authorities. If we know a crime was committed, we are obligated to report it. It is not up to us to decide the consequences of someone's sin or protect them from the consequences. A truly repentant person should be willing to face the consequences of their sin.

Regardless of the consequences, perpetrators of sexual harm are not without hope of salvation. God's mercy extends even to them. To God, sin is sin. Sure, there may be differences in its effects, but ALL sin separates us from God. And, as David confessed, all sin is against God. Jesus's payment for sin was effective for everyone and every sin. So, if an abuser or rapist or murderer believes in Jesus and repents, their sin is removed. Micah 7:19 puts it, "He will again have compassion on us; he will tread our iniquities underfoot. You will cast all our sins into the depths of the sea." Even now, in 2025, man has not reached to the uttermost depths of the sea. It's just another way of saying that God has completely removed our sin from us.

Although this story focuses heavily on David's sin, it's encouraging to remember his repentant heart in Psalm 51. He wants to have his joy restored. He wants to teach others God's ways. He wants a clean heart and a renewed spirit.

David was a man who loved deeply and served his God with a whole heart, despite his sin. He was a forerunner of Jesus, a type of Christ, although a flawed one.

John Piper, founder and teacher of Desiring God, puts it this way:

> It all circles back to Christ. The only hope that David would ever have that he could be forgiven and be happily in heaven with Uriah and Bathsheba and a holy God is that Jesus Christ lived and served and died in a way radically different than David. All of us depend totally on the upside-down way that Jesus used his infinite power on the cross.[12]

What Does Forgiveness for a Victim of Sexual Abuse Look Like?

David's heart of repentance and God's forgiveness is a beautiful thing, but what does forgiveness between victim and perpetrator look like? Anger, resentment, indignation, and outrage are all normal and appropriate responses to abuse. Forgiveness is also appropriate, but it's not normal. It doesn't naturally flow out of the heart of a victim of abuse. Forgiveness takes work, and it takes time. As Christians, our goal is to be conformed to Jesus. His heart is forgiving, so our hearts should be as well. We forgive because he has forgiven us. He is our example. For the Christian, forgiveness is not optional. But it's not easy either.

Forgiveness is not a feeling, it's an action. We don't wait until we feel we can forgive before offering forgiveness. That's where the work comes in. If an offender asks for forgiveness, we need to offer it because that is what God requires. Since no one could sin against us to the extent we have sinned against God, we have no right to withhold forgiveness, even if we don't feel we are ready to forgive. We follow his example.

With time and work, the feeling will come. What forgiveness does is release the offender from the debt of the harm they caused us. In doing that, we will also keep ourselves from resentment and bitterness.

You could say there are stages to forgiveness. For some, the first stage will be forgiving the offender, and the second stage is working on their heart to truly forgive. Others will flip the stages, having done the heart work first and then ready to offer forgiveness if the offender repents. Still others may never have the opportunity to offer forgiveness but can still do the heart work. When you can truly think of the one who sinned against you without any malice or bitterness and pray for them in a positive way (for their success, not just for conviction), then I think your heart is where it ought to be—ready to forgive. You have done the work of forgiveness, even though the one who sinned may never ask for your forgiveness.

The method we use in forgiving needs to be appropriate. Matthew 18:15-17 is not the blueprint for the process of an abuse victim forgiving a perpetrator. It may be too damaging and/or dangerous for a victim to confront the perpetrator alone. This is where time comes in. A survivor should make sure they are in a good, solid emotional and spiritual place before confronting their abuser. Again, look at the whole of Scripture when thinking about interactions between a survivor and abuser. Look at how God expects his people to show justice and protection to the vulnerable (Psalm 82:3-4; Proverbs 31:8-9). Forcing them to face their abuser and/or quickly forgive them does not accomplish that.

Many survivors can see themselves in Bathsheba's story. They were victims of sexual harm, but blamed for it. Some were not believed when they said harm took place, especially if the abuser was their own husband or a beloved leader. They may need to hear over and over that it was not their fault. And they should be encouraged by Bathsheba's story because God's restoration is for them too.

What is God's heart for Bathsheba?

Restoration – In this narrative we see two kinds of restoration. We see David's restoration from sin—a restored relationship with God, restored joy, and restored heart. For Bathsheba, we see the kind of restoration that comes from brokenness—like the healing of a broken bone, something that was restored to full strength and use after being damaged. What type of restoration do you need?

* As a sixteen-year-old brand-new Christian, I devoured the Bible. When I read the book of Joel, I felt like it was speaking directly to me, right into the effects of abuse on my life. My abuse had ended about a year before, and I saw the locusts that destroyed Israel as abuse, shame, fear, and despair in my life. What one had left behind, the next one took. But God says in Joel 2:25, "I will restore to you the years that the swarming locust has eaten." Hope flooded my soul. I took it as a promise, and God has been faithful in fulfilling it. It struck me that God didn't owe me anything, but he wanted to restore those lost years out of his great love and mercy. Read Joel 2:23–27. What were the "locusts" in your life? How have you experienced God's restoration?

* Psalm 34:18 – God is near to the brokenhearted and saves those crushed in spirit. Bathsheba surely was brokenhearted following the death of her husband and child. God cared about her heart, and he cares about our hearts. God restores broken hearts when we lean into him. There is a nearness that comes from suffering that maybe can't be found any other way. How have you felt the nearness of God as you have worked through your suffering?

* Because of God's grace and heart of restoration, it is possible to come out of suffering stronger than before. Read 1 Peter 5:10. In what ways do you want God to restore, confirm, strengthen, and establish you? Ask God to accomplish them and trust that he will.

How can we apply the lessons from Bathsheba's story?

Breaking the silence.

* People knew of David's sin/crimes and didn't come forward or confront him. Sexual abuse flourishes in silence and darkness (see Isaiah 29:15). Why do you think none of David's entourage confronted him? Why do people today not confront abusers? What good could have happened if someone had told David what he wanted to do was wrong?

* Nathan had the courage to expose David's sin. Nathan was a prophet, a man of God. His fear of God outweighed his fear of the king. He should be an example for all of us who call ourselves Christians.

How have you been courageous in your story or someone else's?

* Believe the unbelievable. David was a charismatic hero, not someone we would think could sexually harm another. This is typical of predators today. They are good at that persona. They work at it so that if an accusation is made, no one will believe it. (I'm not saying David did that, just that it might've been hard to believe that he had hurt someone.) Predators charm their way into positions of trust. They are well-liked, charismatic, friendly, and appear trustworthy. They are pastors, coaches, teachers, police officers, scout masters, choir directors, babysitters, fathers, husbands—the list goes on because they could be anyone. That's what makes it hard to recognize them: they look and act like everybody else. Can you think of someone who was convicted of a sexual crime when it seemed impossible that they were guilty?

* Be discerning. Warning signs for sexual predators include secrets, isolation, gifts, grooming techniques, and more.

* If you feel uncomfortable around someone or see red flags, tell someone or report them to your local authority. If you know about abuse of a child, report it. I think you should go one step further. Confront the abuser, like Nathan did. Most abusers are cowards, which is one reason they operate in secret. Reports to authorities may not go anywhere. But if you tell an abuser that you're aware of what they are doing and are watching, that may be enough to stop the abuse. And that is worth one uncomfortable conversation.

It was not your fault—reprise.

* Bathsheba suffered greatly: sexual harm, the death of her husband, the death of her child—none of which was her fault. She was a victim and should be treated that way. Many women today have been sexually harmed by someone they trusted, even husbands or boyfriends. Their harm is sometimes misunderstood or discounted or they are blamed. They didn't feel free from it until someone told them it wasn't their fault. If you were a victim of sexual abuse, it was not your fault. Do you believe that?

Chapter Five
God's Heart of Love:
Tamar – Listening to the Voiceless

Tamar's Story

2 Samuel 13:1–22

Now Absalom, David's son, had a beautiful sister, whose name was Tamar. And after a time Amnon, David's son, loved her. And Amnon was so tormented that he made himself ill because of his sister Tamar, for she was a virgin, and it seemed impossible to Amnon to do anything to her. But Amnon had a friend, whose name was Jonadab, the son of Shimeah, David's brother. And Jonadab was a very crafty man. And he said to him, "O son of the king, why are you so haggard morning after morning? Will you not tell me?" Amnon said to him, "I love Tamar, my brother Absalom's sister." Jonadab said to him, "Lie down on your bed and pretend to be ill. And when your father comes to see you, say to him, 'Let my sister Tamar come and give me bread to eat, and prepare the food in my sight, that I may see it and eat it from her hand.'" So Amnon lay down and pretended to be ill. And when the king came to see him, Amnon said to the king, "Please let my sister Tamar come and make a couple of cakes in my sight, that I may eat from her hand."

Then David sent home to Tamar, saying, "Go to your brother Amnon's house and prepare food for him." So Tamar went to her brother Amnon's house, where he was lying down. And she took dough and kneaded it and made cakes in his sight and baked the cakes. And she took the pan and emptied it out before him, but he refused to eat. And Amnon said, "Send out everyone from me." So everyone went out from him. Then Amnon said to Tamar, "Bring the food into the chamber, that I may eat from your hand." And Tamar took the cakes she had made and brought them into the chamber to Amnon her brother. But when she brought them near him to eat, he took hold of her and said to her, "Come, lie with me, my sister." She answered him, "No, my brother, do not violate me, for such a thing is not done in Israel; do not do this outrageous thing. As for me, where could I carry my shame? And as for you, you would be as one of the outrageous fools in Israel. Now therefore, please speak to the king, for he will not withhold me from you." But he would not listen to her, and being stronger than she, he violated her and lay with her.

Then Amnon hated her with very great hatred, so that the hatred with which he hated her was greater than the love with which he had loved her. And Amnon said to her, "Get up! Go!" But she said to him, "No, my brother, for this wrong in sending me away is greater than the other that you did to me." But he would not listen to her. He called the young man who served him and said, "Put this woman out of my presence and bolt the door after her." Now she was wearing a long robe with sleeves, for thus were the virgin daughters of the king dressed. So his servant put her out and bolted the door after her. And Tamar put ashes on her head and tore the long robe that she wore. And she laid her hand on her head and went away, crying aloud as she went. And her brother Absalom said to her, "Has Amnon your brother been with you? Now hold your peace, my sister. He is your brother; do not take this to heart." So Tamar lived, a desolate woman, in her brother Absalom's house. When King David heard of all these things, he was very angry. But Absalom spoke to Amnon neither good nor bad, for Absalom hated Amnon, because he had violated his sister Tamar.

2 Samuel 13:1–22

Who Was Tamar?

In this chapter, we look at one of the more known and taught stories of sexual harm in the Bible: the rape of David's daughter, Tamar. A story where sexual harm and its effects are the main points, it opens by introducing the two main characters: Tamar, the beautiful sister of Amnon, David's son. And Amnon, who loved her.

It sounds lovely, a brother who loves his sister. But in the next sentence, we learn that Amnon's love for his sister isn't the pure sibling love we would hope for. It says Amnon was so tormented because of his sister that he made himself sick. His torment was because Tamar "was a virgin, and it seemed impossible to Amnon to do anything to her" (v. 2). I should point out that Tamar wasn't the cause of Amnon's torment; it was his lust. It was his own sin that made him sick.

This is a bad news/good news situation. The bad news is that Amnon had a sinful attraction to his sister. The good news is that it initially seemed impossible to him to act on it. This is what any sin should seem like to a Christian. Some sin we need to wrestle with until the life is choked out of it. Amnon seemed to be in a battle against his sinful desire, and then, in walked his friend. Instead of helping him shut the door to his sin, he swung the door open wider. We don't need friends like that; we're already bent toward sin.

Amnon's friend came up with a plan to get Amnon what he wanted. It involved deception—a lot of it. He had to deceive his father, King David; the servants in his house; and his sister, Tamar. This wasn't a sin he just stumbled into without thinking. It was thought-out and premeditated, with every detail planned and prepared beforehand. There were numerous places along the way where Amnon could have stopped the snowball of sin in its tracks, but he didn't. It just kept rolling on, growing bigger with each deception.

The Wisdom of Tamar vs. The Foolishness of Amnon

Amnon took his friend's advice. He pretended to be ill and lay down on his bed. King David went to him, and Amnon asked David to send Tamar to make food for him. David did what Amnon asked. Tamar came to his house and prepared food for him. He then dismissed the servants and asked Tamar to come into his bedchamber and feed him the food from her hand. Cue suspenseful music.

As Amnon is forcing himself on her, Tamar offers a legal and moral alternative. But Amnon is too committed to his sinful plan to consider her advice. Tamar's answer has so much wisdom in it.

First and foremost, she said no, and she reminded her brother who they were—Israelites, a set-apart people who should live according to God's law. She even used the same wording we saw in the story of the Levite's concubine in Judges 19. "Outrageous," and, "Such a thing is not done in Israel." Of course, Amnon knew what he was doing was sinful, but at this point, he didn't care. He wanted what he wanted, and Tamar's appeal to righteousness fell on deaf ears. In Jeremiah 5:21–22, God seems to echo Tamar: "Hear this, O foolish and senseless people, who have eyes, but see not, and have ears, but hear not. Do you not fear me? declares the LORD. Do you not tremble before me?"

The first appeal Tamar made was to the fear of the Lord. That was what she meant when she said, "For such a thing is not done in Israel" (2 Samuel 13:12). Israel belonged to the Lord, and for Amnon to violate God's law by violating her was outrageous to her.

Next, she appealed to how his actions would affect her: "Do not violate me. Where could I carry my shame?" (A paraphrase of v. 13.) Being a virgin forcibly raped by her brother would not just affect her physically. She would carry the shame of losing her virginity in such a violent way for the rest of her life. Tamar appealed to Amnon's love for her as his sister. But his brotherly love for her had been eclipsed by his sinful desires.

Her next appeal was for his own reputation. People would find out what he had done, and he would be considered a fool. Not just your run-of-the-mill fool, but one of the outrageous fools in Israel. This is the type of person who rejects God and his ways and is unwilling to obey him.

With all her reasons obviously making no impact, Tamar resorted to acquiescing to what he wanted, but lawfully. Tamar suggested that Amnon ask David for her to be his wife. Since they were half-siblings, this would have been allowed. But Amnon was beyond reason: "But he would not listen to her, and being stronger than she, he violated her and lay with her" (2 Samuel 13:14).

Think about what's being said there. It was all about him. He wouldn't listen to her. Tamar was filled with wise counsel and even a righteous way to get Amnon what he wanted, yet he wouldn't listen to her. That tells us where his heart was. He was quick to listen to the voice of evil from his friend but not the voice of wisdom. That shows his rejection of God and his utter foolishness.

Amnon was stronger than Tamar. This tells us a couple of things. It reminds us that all abuse is an abuse of power. The difference in physical strength between men and women is a common power imbalance and is part of the story here. This also tells us that Tamar probably tried to get away from him. Why else would the Bible need to tell us that he was stronger? Either she was fighting back, which is likely, or she was so threatened by his physical power over her that she submitted to him.

Either way, he violated her and lay with her. This says the same thing in two ways. Scripture does that to emphasize a point. This was the completion of Amnon allowing sin to rule over him. Even though he heard truth and a way of escape, he rejected it and listened instead to evil. And getting what he so desperately wanted satisfied him and caused him to love her more deeply, right? Wrong. "Then Amnon hated her with very great hatred, so that the hatred with which he hated her was greater than the love with which he had loved her. And Amnon said to her, 'Get up! Go!'" (v. 15).

How about that? A sinful act didn't give him the result he thought it would. Remember, Amnon loved his sister at the beginning of the story. He probably thought having sex with her would not just satisfy him but be a dream come true. The dream became a nightmare. That's what sin does. That's what Satan does. He takes what God created to be beautiful and satisfying, and he twists it into something violent and ugly. It shouldn't surprise us that Amnon ends up hating Tamar. Sin is a fool. It rejects God. It denies God. It despises God and everyone reflecting the image of God.

Amnon threw Tamar out. He didn't even want her in his presence, she so disgusted him. The one he should have hated was himself. Tamar was an innocent victim. She did nothing to deserve his violence or animosity. She even begged him not to throw her out because that would be even worse than what he had already done. Even at that point, she was willing to become his wife to cover his sin and her shame. But he rejected her. She left and tore the sleeves of her garment. This was a symbol that she was no longer a virgin. He had taken something from her that she would never be able to take back.

Tamar Is Silenced

Next, her brother Absalom found her and somehow knew that Amnon had been with her. We don't know how that information reached him, but whether it was something he had suspected would happen or someone told him, he gave her bad advice. He said, "Has Amnon your brother been with you? Now hold your peace, my sister. He is your brother; do not take this to heart" (v. 20).

This is so prevalent in our culture too. Often when abuse happens within a family, the victim is told not to say anything. It will just cause more problems within the family. It was your brother. He didn't mean anything by it. Just let it go. Boys will be boys. Move on, don't talk about it, don't take it to heart. In other words, don't let it bother you. How ridiculous! Sexual violence can affect a young person for the rest of their life. Look at what happened with Tamar.

Verse 21 says that Tamar lived, a desolate woman, in her brother Absalom's house. This indicates that Tamar lived the *rest of her life* as a desolate woman. Desolate means without hope. So many victims can relate to this. Having their voices silenced, they can't find healing. Everyone wants them to forget it and move on, but facing it and talking about it is necessary for healing. It would be like swimming against a strong current and being told to just move forward. It's almost impossible. The harder you try, the more tired your muscles become until you give up and are swept away. Tamar lived her life without hope. The only thing she had going for her was that she was the daughter of the king, so she was at least cared for and didn't have to fend for herself to stay alive.

We also learn the king's reaction. Verse 21 says, "When King David heard of all these things, he was very angry." But it doesn't give any indication he did anything about it. I suppose it was good he was angry, but where was the love for his children that would have included consequences for Amnon? David didn't have the greatest parenting skills, at least not with his adult children.

Wrong Reactions to Sexual Harm Lead to More Harm

But, again, this is the typical reaction of a parent to sexual violence within their family. They may be angry, devastated, and hurt, but they may not react appropriately—protecting and caring for the victim. They may make excuses and support the one who did reprehensible harm. And they may not seek justice for their child who was harmed, but do all they can to keep the world from finding out what has happened in their family.

Other parents go too far the other way, which is what Absalom did. He let his hatred for what Amnon did grow to the point that he waited for a chance to kill him. Two years later, he did just that. Some parents say things like, "If my child is ever abused, I'll kill the guy." In cases of abuse, we need to remember that abused children most often have a relationship with their abuser. The abuser may be a family member or a friend or a coach or a teacher—someone they love and care about. A father or brother saying they will kill an abuser may lead the victim to remain silent about the abuse. We need to be careful about how we talk about abusers and how we treat victims.

The royal family handled the sexual harm of Tamar poorly. We should expect more from those in power. God is very clear about the responsibility of the powerful to protect the powerless. In advice to the king in Proverbs 31:8–9, we find, "Open your mouth for the mute, for the rights of all who are destitute. Open your mouth, judge righteously, defend the rights of the poor and needy." Abuse victims are among the mute and destitute. Isn't that exactly how Tamar ended up?

"Hold your peace."

"She lived as a desolate woman."

The king, and anyone else with any power, should have defended her rights and opened their mouths, but they didn't.

Paul weighs in too, in Ephesians 5:3–5, 11:

But sexual immorality and all impurity or covetousness must not even be named among you, as is proper among saints. Let there be no filthiness nor foolish talk nor crude joking, which are out of place, but instead let there be thanksgiving. For you may be sure of this, that everyone who is sexually immoral or impure, or who is covetous (that is, an idolater), has no inheritance in the kingdom of Christ and God. Take no part in the unfruitful works of darkness, but instead expose them.

When Paul says sexual immorality shouldn't be named among us, he wasn't saying to keep silent about it. He was saying it has no place in the life of someone who is walking in love, as Christ loved us. But he also says walking as children of light should expose the works of darkness. That's what Christians and the church should be doing when they learn of sexual abuse—unlike David, who got angry but did nothing. We should get angry, expose the darkness, love and protect victims, and seek justice.

Generational Abuse

One of the big issues with families who keep silent about abuse is that it becomes a cycle of generational abuse. David had an issue with sex. It manifested in his having multiple wives and concubines and peaked with his abuse of Bathsheba and the murder of her husband. Then his offspring continued the same sin pattern. Solomon's sex drive is well-documented with hundreds of wives who turned him from the God of his father to following after their gods. Amnon raped his sister. Absalom murdered his brother.

Ironically, it was David who said:

> "How blessed is he whose wrongdoing is forgiven,
>
> Whose sin is covered!
>
> How blessed is a person whose guilt the LORD does not take into account,
>
> And in whose spirit there is no deceit!
>
> When I kept silent about my sin, my body wasted away
>
> Through my groaning all day long.
>
> I acknowledged my sin to You,
>
> And I did not hide my guilt;
>
> I said, 'I will confess my wrongdoings to the LORD';
>
> And You forgave the guilt of my sin."
>
> Psalm 32:1–3, 5 NASB

Keeping silent about sin doesn't just cause problems for the one who sinned. It also hurts the one sinned against. Tamar lived a desolate life in her brother's house, where she was told to keep silent. She lived a life of shame, while her brother Absalom's silence stoked his hatred, leading to more sin and more division in the family.

Tamar lost her voice, power, and relationships.

According to sexual abuse expert Dr. Diane Langberg, victims of sexual abuse lose their voice, power, and relationships.[13] It's easy to see how those three things were manifested in Tamar's story.

Think about what it means to live as a "desolate" woman. Her voice was silenced by Absalom. She couldn't tell her story. Without her voice, there was no hope of justice being done. Without talking about it, she couldn't overcome her shame.

Her power was taken from her by both Amnon when he raped her and Absalom when he told her to keep silent about it. Absalom may have had right motives. Perhaps he thought Tamar would be better off if she didn't talk about the rape. But keeping her silent in his house only took her power away. She had no control over her own life.

She also lost her relationships. Tamar asked Amnon, "Where could I carry my shame?" After he raped her, Amnon hated her. She lost her relationship with her brother and probably other family members, but she also lost future relationships. She hid herself away and didn't have a chance for a loving marriage relationship.

What is God's heart for Tamar?

Love – God's love is for everyone but maybe is seen most powerfully in the poor and needy. Psalm 109 talks about that. "But you, O God my Lord, deal on my behalf for your name's sake; because your steadfast love is good, deliver me! For I am poor and needy, and my heart is stricken within me" (vv. 21–22). Read the rest of the Psalm. How does it inform you about God's love for Tamar? Do you see yourself in any of the descriptions?

* God's forgiveness stems from his love for us. Look at Micah 7:18 and John 3:16. How would you describe the depth of God's love?

* Based on Romans 8:39 and thinking of Tamar, can any suffering keep you from God's love?

* How can you find God's love even in difficult circumstances? (See 2 Thessalonians 3:5; Romans 5:5.)

* How should we treat one another as God's children? (See 1 John 4:7–8.)

How can we apply the lessons from Tamar's story?

Restore Voice, Power, and Relationship

In the foreword of Mary DeMuth's *We Too: How the Church Can Respond Redemptively to the Sexual Abuse Crisis*, pastor J.D. Greear writes:

> Where should the church begin to address the crisis among us? By listening. Listening does at least two things. First, listening restores voice and dignity to the survivor. During abuse, voice is ignored. Or marginalized. Or silenced outright. After abuse, a sense of voice is often lost. A church that does not listen communicates that what a survivor experienced doesn't matter to God or God's people. Second, listening removes ignorance from the church and church leaders. We need to understand as much as survivors need to be heard. Ignorance on our part makes us ill-equipped to be ambassadors of Christ. Survivors of abuse are in every one of our congregations. Potential victims are, too. How tragic if we neglect to protect them because our ears were found closed?[14]

* We can help restore the voice of a survivor by listening to them. Allow them to share their stories, remind them it wasn't their fault, and encourage them to learn of God's heart through his Word (his voice written down).

* We can help restore a survivor's power by allowing them to take control of their lives in decision-making, finding and using their gifts, and making sure our churches are places they can feel safe and cared for.

* We can help restore relationships by showing them love, being trustworthy friends, and including them in the life of the church. Most importantly, encourage them to have a growing relationship with Jesus.

Take on generational abuse.

Amnon is what we call today a familial predator, someone who preys on their own family members. This is such a difficult type of abuse for several reasons. Abuse perpetrated by people who should love the victim can be especially traumatizing. Some family members protect the abusers. Other family members don't want to believe one of their own could cause such harm. And victims are less likely to disclose abuse.

In We Too: How the Church Can Respond Redemptively to the Sexual Abuse Crisis, author Mary DeMuth says:

> So often, sexual assault happens in a context in which the perpetrator is stronger or has more power in the relationship. Fear of what others will think, particularly when the abuse happens within the family structure also keeps survivors silent. No one wants to be the reason for a family's downfall. No one wants to be the linchpin that, when pulled out, unhinges a religious system that is otherwise intact. No one wants to get people in trouble, even if it is necessary to protect yourself.[15]

If you were abused by a family member, I am so sorry for all you've suffered. This must be an especially difficult chapter for you to study, but nothing is hopeless with God. The abundant life Jesus offers is for all of his followers, even those with the worst stories. I pray that you will trust him and know the depths of his love for you.

A few years back, I spoke with a woman who had been violently raped by her brother repeatedly. She experienced the same sort of treatment from her family that Tamar did. She was told to keep silent, that the family would handle it privately, and that getting authorities involved would only make things worse and divide the family. Her family sacrificed her well-being to save face.

Let's not forget, this was a crime. Family members who knew what was happening were obligated by law to turn her brother in to the authorities. He was the one who was at fault for hurting the family. Had they not kept silent, she could have gotten the help she needed much earlier in life, and other victims could have been kept from harm.

When we spoke, this woman was in her sixties and was still dealing with the trauma of the abuse and of being silenced. My heart broke for her. By the end of our weekend, after hearing several times that the abuse was not her fault and being encouraged to share as much of her story as she could with someone, she told me she was beginning to feel like healing was possible. She was right—it is. If you're reading this and wondering if healing really is possible, I encourage you to find a support group, a coach, or a counselor with whom you feel safe, and, in that context, work on healing.

* What steps are you taking toward healing?

Chapter Six
God's Heart of Protection:
Esther – Where Was God?

Esther's Story
Esther 2:1-4, 12-18

After these things, when the anger of King Ahasuerus had abated, he remembered Vashti and what she had done and what had been decreed against her. Then the king's young men who attended him said, "Let beautiful young virgins be sought out for the king. And let the king appoint officers in all the provinces of his kingdom to gather all the beautiful young virgins to the harem in Susa the citadel, under custody of Hegai, the king's eunuch, who is in charge of the women. Let their cosmetics be given them. And let the young woman who pleases the king be queen instead of Vashti." This pleased the king, and he did so.

. . . Now when the turn came for each young woman to go in to King Ahasuerus, after being twelve months under the regulations for the women, since this was the regular period of their beautifying, six months with oil of myrrh and six months with spices and ointments for women—when the young woman went in to the king in this way, she was given whatever she desired to take with her from the harem to the king's palace. In the evening she would go in, and in the morning she would return to the second harem in custody of Shaashgaz, the king's eunuch, who was in charge of the concubines. She would not go in to the king again, unless the king delighted in her and she was summoned by name.

When the turn came for Esther the daughter of Abihail

the uncle of Mordecai, who had taken her as his own daughter, to go in to the king, she asked for nothing except what Hegai the king's eunuch, who had charge of the women, advised. Now Esther was winning favor in the eyes of all who saw her. And when Esther was taken to King Ahasuerus, into his royal palace, in the tenth month, which is the month of Tebeth, in the seventh year of his reign, the king loved Esther more than all the women, and she won grace and favor in his sight more than all the virgins, so that he set the royal crown on her head and made her queen instead of Vashti. Then the king gave a great feast for all his officials and servants; it was Esther's feast. He also granted a remission of taxes to the provinces and gave gifts with royal generosity.

Esther 2:1–4, 12–18

Who Was Esther?

The story of Esther has all the marks of a modern-day mini-series: royalty, beautiful women, political tension, mystery, plot twists, murder, justice, and lots of sex. But it was not a made-for-TV show with a goal of high ratings and even higher commercial sales. It was a real-life drama, starring a young woman God used to save his people at great personal cost.

Before Esther became queen of Persia, she was an orphaned girl, raised by her older cousin, Mordecai. In spite of her tragic circumstances at a young age, she grew into a beautiful young woman. Her outward appearance was matched by her inward grace and godly spirit. Then, as she neared the age of marriage (and I imagine with her inner and outer beauty, there were guys lining up to ask Mordecai for her hand), her life was turned upside down once again.

The Truth About Becoming Queen

The king, Ahasuerus, banished his queen for not obeying him when he commanded her to appear before him and his guests to show off her beauty. No one denied the king, not even his queen. Plus, he was pressured by the guests, who were leaders of neighboring countries. They were afraid their own wives would take her lead. So, Queen Vashti was out, and the king needed a new queen. The way he went about finding one was not what we might expect, although it sounds a lot like what happened in *Cinderella* when the prince held a ball to find a wife.

Except this was not a ball. And it was not a beauty contest. If you grew up with VeggieTales, you might think that's all it was. I'm sure the writers were just trying to make an X-rated story into something closer to a G rating, more appropriate for kids' viewing. And I don't really have a problem with that. As with anything we teach kids, we need to teach at their level, using words and concepts they can understand. But it will become a problem if we never tell them the whole truth of Esther's story.

The main message of the book of Esther, after all, is the saving of God's people. But as adults, we can't ignore the sexual harm that Esther went through to be the conduit God used. It's important to teach the truth because it's how God chose to accomplish his plans. He could have done it another way, but Esther being forced into a sexual relationship with the king was what he used. We must not miss what is there for us to learn.

It started with rounding up beautiful virgins. This is what we would call a power predator, if we were talking about criminal activity in today's world. A power predator uses force to coerce someone into a sexual relationship. That is exactly what the king was doing. The young virgins didn't have a choice. They couldn't say no. They were taken for the king. This sounds like the definition of sex trafficking. There is no indication in the book of Esther that the other virgins were released once the king made his choice. Rather, it indicates they were added to his harem.

There was a process. They didn't come into the king's palace, bake their best chocolate chip cookie, and have the king pick the winner. There were preparations that took twelve months with ointments and perfumes. That part doesn't sound so bad—a year of spa treatment, making your skin feel and smell fabulous. But then comes the real purpose. Would they please the king? No, not in the bathing suit, evening gown, and talent competitions. They needed to please him sexually, each one spending the night with the king.

They could take whatever they wanted with them when they went in to the king. Esther asked the king's eunuch for advice. He knew the king's sexual preferences, and Esther was wise to follow his advice. She could have chosen not to do what was expected—in essence, "throw" her night with the king—and just end up in the "second harem" and maybe not have sex with the king again. But she looked to the wisdom of Mordecai and the eunuch for her best chance to not just survive, but also to please the king. And she did please him. Whatever she did, the sex she had with the king pleased him above all the others, and Esther was made queen.

I am sure being queen had its perks. We see further into the story that she had a staff who could put on a feast. Her living accommodations were above average, and manual labor was a thing of the past. As far as women in that culture, she had more power than most. And the spa treatments most likely continued—she still had to please the king, after all.

But she didn't have freedom. She wasn't free to marry a man of her choice. She wasn't free to have sex that was pleasing to her. She wasn't free to say no. If she was called by the king, she had to go and please him, regardless of how she was feeling or what she wanted. Additionally, she couldn't go before the king, unless he summoned her, without risking death. Even with the perks, it doesn't seem like a life most women would want, then or now.

The Why Questions

Two of the most-asked questions by women who have been sexually harmed are, "Why did God allow this to happen?" and "Why didn't God stop it or keep it from happening?" The book of Esther is a good place for survivors to look for answers. In fact, Mordecai gives an answer to those questions without Esther even asking them. He said to her, "Who knows if you have come to this kingdom for such a time as this?" (paraphrase of v. 14).

Mordecai realized that Esther was in a position to save the entire Jewish race. Perhaps he had pondered the "why" questions as well. Wouldn't you, if it were your child? And now the answer seems obvious. How else could there have been a person in the right position at the right time to stop the slaughter of the Jews ordered by the king? You may argue, "But why an innocent young girl? Couldn't God have raised Mordecai to a position of power to do the same?" God could have, but he chose another way. And because of the way he chose, there is so much more to glean than just a courageous Jew who stood up for his people.

In Esther's story, the victim becomes the hero. The meek and lowly girl becomes strong and powerful. The least among us becomes the greatest. Do any of those themes sound familiar? Maybe found in the Bible's overarching story—the story of Jesus? Jesus was beaten and bruised for our sins. He became a man, meek and lowly, to take our place. He was humble. But at the right time, having accomplished his purpose of saving his people, he was exalted. Jesus knew abuse. He was acquainted with suffering. But he endured it "for the joy that was set before him" (Hebrews 12:2)—our salvation, God's plan for him from the beginning. In a parallel way, it was God's plan for Esther to save her people.

When Jesus hung on the cross and cried, "My God, my God, why have you forsaken me?" (Matthew 27:46), I don't think he was asking, "Why, God?" or feeling that God had abandoned him. I think he was calling to mind Psalm 22, a psalm the crowd of Jews watching him probably would have known. This psalm vividly foreshadowed that moment, with his garments being divided by lot (v. 18), the mocking he endured (vv. 6–8), and even the piercing of his hands and feet (v. 16). But he knew the outcome. He knew his God was with him and would never forsake him (v. 24). The same is true for all who have suffered sexual harm (or any other harm) and wondered, where was God?

God was right there.

Every "why?" is different, except that every suffering has a purpose. It could be the purpose is obvious, or it could be that we will not know it in this life. But rest assured: because it happened, it had a purpose.

Entrusted With Suffering

What if we looked at the suffering in our lives as something God has entrusted to us, like he entrusted the fate of the Jewish nation to Esther? We don't know who might be watching us and our reaction to suffering. You can be sure someone is. What will our reaction to suffering teach others about our God? Ultimately, that is the point of our suffering.

God's Protection

The Bible is full of verses about God being a stronghold, a protector, one who fights for us, hiding us in the shelter of his wings, being a tower we can run to. He calls his people to care for one another. God protects his people. Yet, he also tells us we will be hated and treated unfairly, maybe even put to death on his account. Paul is an example of one who suffered many things, any one of which could have killed him (see 2 Corinthians 11:24–28). It doesn't seem God always protects his people.

Mordecai told Esther not to expose herself as a Jew because it wasn't safe to do so. She followed his advice and became queen. Even then, she kept silent about her heritage until she had to speak up to save her people. She did so after much prayer and fasting—another way to seek God's protection. And finally, she found the courage to say, "If I die, I die."

> And they told Mordecai what Esther had said. Then Mordecai told them to reply to Esther, "Do not think to yourself that in the king's palace you will escape any more than all the other Jews. For if you keep silent at this time, relief and deliverance will rise for the Jews from another place, but you and your father's house will perish. And who knows whether you have not come to the kingdom for such a time as this?" Then Esther told them to reply to Mordecai, "Go, gather all the Jews to be found in Susa, and hold a fast on my behalf, and do not eat or drink for three days, night or day. I and my young women will also fast as you do. Then I will go to the king, though it is against the law, and if I perish, I perish." Mordecai then went away and did everything as Esther had ordered him.
>
> Esther 4:12–17

Yes, God protects his children because he values life. When we are put in unsafe situations, we can trust it is for God's purposes, and we should move ahead with confidence through prayer. While God didn't keep Esther from being taken by the king and didn't keep her from having to perform sexually, that doesn't mean he wasn't protecting her. At least three times in this story, she could have been killed. In that way, God did protect her and at the same time revealed her purpose of saving his people. Even though his plan included putting her in a position of suffering, God had his hand on her to protect her life and accomplish his purposes.

That may be hard for us to understand. But it is something we see throughout Scripture. Think of Job and how much suffering God allowed Satan to inflict on him, although he wasn't allowed to take his life. There's Hosea who God directed to marry a woman he knew would be repeatedly unfaithful. Habakkuk asked God why he wasn't doing anything when Israel had turned from him. God's reply was that he was doing something—working through their heathen enemies to bring about his discipline. And there are many people Jesus healed: the blind man, the bleeding woman, the demon-possessed man, and more. All had suffered for years, to be healed for the glory of God. Ultimately, everything we face is for the glory of God.

Where Was God?

It's interesting that the book of Esther doesn't mention God by name, yet he is there. It's a good example of our own lives. We can't see God, but we can see his hand in our lives. God isn't physically with us, but we can feel his presence. God isn't speaking audibly but we have his Word, Christian friends, and spiritual leaders to guide us. And, for survivors, it may seem that God has abandoned us, but he has not. In fact, he has been with us all along, keeping us safe for our good and his glory.

Satan isn't mentioned in Esther either, but his presence is also obvious. His minion, Haman, is bent on destroying the Jews. Haman's hatred for Mordecai and the Jews is the main plot of the book. His mission against God's people is the same as Satan's—to steal, kill, and destroy (see John 10:10). And he thinks he has accomplished his mission. But the book has not one plot twist, but two.

First, Haman created a plan to kill Mordecai. Mordecai wouldn't bow down to Haman, and this infuriated him. Haman built gallows with a plan to hang Mordecai on them. But the king learned that Mordecai had saved his life by revealing an assassination plot. Instead of hanging Mordecai, Haman stumbled into honoring him in a very public way. His next move was to extinguish the entire Jewish race. But God had his person in place to foil that plan as well.

Esther, with the encouragement and admonishment of Mordecai, intervened for her people and named Haman as the one who had plotted to kill the Jews, including her. The king was furious. Although he could not rescind his order, he allowed the Jews to take up arms and defend themselves. And in the final plot twist, Haman was hanged on the gallows he built for Mordecai. And the wrath of the king was abated.

A Picture of Jesus

At the end of Esther's story, the king gave Haman's house to Esther and Mordecai: "Then Mordecai went out from the presence of the king in royal robes of blue and white, with a great golden crown and a robe of fine linen and purple, and the city of Susa shouted and rejoiced. The Jews had light and gladness and joy and honor" (Esther 8:15–16).

Can you see the parallelism between the story of Esther and the story of Jesus? Even though our focus for this study is on stories of sexual harm and God's heart for those people, we don't want to lose sight of the bigger picture of the Bible. Every book of the Bible is about Jesus. Esther is no exception, from the overall story of saving God's people down to the details of the heroes suffering, being hated, and facing death to accomplish that salvation. It is summed up in Jesus's words in John 10:10: "The thief comes only to steal and kill and destroy. I [Jesus] came that they may have life and have it abundantly."

What is God's heart for Esther?

Protection – God's protection doesn't always look like we think it ought to. We'd like to avoid harm, so that man's sinfulness and the brokenness of the world won't affect us. But that won't happen until Jesus returns and sin is finally and completely eradicated from the earth. In the meantime, evil is at work but restrained by God's protection.

✻   Read Psalm 91. It focuses on God's protection even when circumstances are chaotic and dangerous. Verse 10 says, "No evil shall be allowed to befall you." Considering the rest of the Psalm and Esther's story, how can you trust in God's protection?

* Fear is common for survivors of abuse. How would knowing God protects his children help combat fear? (See Psalm 27; Deut. 31:6; Proverbs 18:10; Isaiah 41:10.)

* God promises to protect his own from evil. (See Psalm 121:7-8.) How would this apply to Esther and to you?

* God will allow suffering in our lives to teach us to trust him and to show himself faithful. What have you learned about God through suffering? (See 2 Corinthians 12:9; Exodus 14:14; Psalm 138:7; Isaiah 54:17; 2 Timothy 2:13; Hebrews 10:23.)

* Esther survived her sexual harm, but others may not. Derek Thomas of Ligonier Ministries says the angels in Psalm 91 will take us "all the way home."[16] They will escort us to heaven when our stories are done. God's protection is over us until the end. In the case of a victim not surviving, how is God faithful in protecting them?

How can we apply the lessons from Esther's story?

The most common questions survivors ask are "Where was God?" and "Why did God allow this?" We may not be able to give an exact answer to those questions—they may be different for each person, but we do have some answers from God's Word.

Where Was God?

* The book of Esther is a perfect place to look for the answer, because God is not mentioned at all in the entire book. Yet, he is so obviously there, guiding, protecting, and saving—not just Esther and Mordecai, but the entire nation of Israel. And there is a clear foreshadowing of Jesus as well. So, the answer is, "He was right there with you." Can you see God in your story?

* Because God is omnipresent (everywhere at all times), he had to be present in your story—all of it—whether you felt his presence or not. As Christians, we have God's Holy Spirit living within us. He doesn't ever leave us. He is within us at all times, even when we sin or when we are sinned against. He is still there. There is nowhere that he is not. (See Psalm 139:7-12; Psalm 100:5; John 14:16-17.)

Answering the Question: Why?

In this life, we may never know the "why" of our harm. But we can trust that God has a purpose in all that we suffer. Here are a few answers to the "why" question:

* The book of Job – Amid losing everything, Job learned to suffer well and to trust God even in great loss.

* Mark 5:1–19 – After Jesus delivered him, the demon-possessed man begged to go with Jesus. But Jesus told him to stay. In verse 19, Jesus told him why (his purpose): "Go home to your friends and tell them how much the Lord has done for you, and how he has had mercy on you."

* Mark 5:25–34 – The bleeding woman endured physical and financial suffering for a prolonged amount of time, as a social outcast, all to declare the power of Jesus.

* 2 Corinthians 1:3–7 – We are told to comfort others with the comfort we have received from God.

* Romans 8:28–29 – We are told that not only will God use our suffering for our good and his glory, but he will use it to conform us to the image of his Son—the ultimate goal of every Christian.

* Isaiah 45:3 – We see that God hides treasure in dark places, that we might know him. Stars are always in the sky but are most visible in the dark. The darker the sky, the more visible the stars. This chapter touched on some very hard concepts—God doesn't just use difficult circumstances, but ordains them; he can stop bad things from happening but sometimes doesn't; protection might look very different than we think it should, etc... Take some time to consider and pray about the things that were difficult for you. How do these things inform your understanding of God's heart?

Quick Note

The stories we will explore from the New Testament have a common thread. That thread is finding freedom from the past. Unlike most of the women we've studied thus far, these women may not have been victims of sexual harm. Their stories stem from their own struggles with sexual sin. We will look at three different women, three different stories, but all of them have two things in common: a shameful sexual past and an encounter with Jesus. I pray you find the same encouragement and freedom that Jesus offered to them.

Dane Ortlund has this to say about God's heart for the Samaritan woman and other outcasts, "For the outcast, from the nation of Israel to individuals like the woman at the well. God loves, protects, pursues, heals, restores, and exalts outcasts. He even uses them to further his kingdom: "The heart of God hearkens toward those who have been sexually exploited. Consider the myriad passages about the quartet of the vulnerable (widows, orphans, the poor, and aliens) throughout the biblical narrative—God is concerned for the downtrodden, and he punishes those who oppress the least of these."[17]

God is for Me

Chapter Seven
God's Heart of Grace:
The Samaritan Woman – Shame and Guilt

The Samaritan Woman's Story

John 4:1–42

Now when Jesus learned that the Pharisees had heard that Jesus was making and baptizing more disciples than John (although Jesus himself did not baptize, but only his disciples), he left Judea and departed again for Galilee. And he had to pass through Samaria. So he came to a town of Samaria called Sychar, near the field that Jacob had given to his son Joseph. Jacob's well was there; so Jesus, wearied as he was from his journey, was sitting beside the well. It was about the sixth hour.

A woman from Samaria came to draw water. Jesus said to her, "Give me a drink." (For his disciples had gone away into the city to buy food.) The Samaritan woman said to him, "How is it that you, a Jew, ask for a drink from me, a woman of Samaria?" (For Jews have no dealings with Samaritans.) Jesus answered her, "If you knew the gift of God, and who it is that is saying to you, 'Give me a drink,' you would have asked him, and he would have given you living water." The woman said to him, "Sir, you have nothing to draw water with, and the well is deep. Where do you get that living water? Are you greater than our father Jacob? He gave us the well and drank from it himself, as did his sons and his livestock." Jesus said to her, "Everyone who drinks of this water will be thirsty again, but whoever drinks of the water that I will give him will never be thirsty again. The water that I will give him will become in him a spring of water welling up to eternal life." The woman said to him, "Sir, give me this water, so that I will not be thirsty or have to come here to draw water."

Jesus said to her, "Go, call your husband, and come here." The woman answered him, "I have no husband." Jesus said to her, "You are right in saying, 'I have no husband'; for you have had five husbands, and the one you now have is not your husband. What you have said is true." The woman said to him, "Sir, I perceive that you are a prophet. Our fathers worshiped on this mountain, but you say that in Jerusalem is the place where people ought to worship." Jesus said to her, "Woman, believe me, the hour is coming when neither on this mountain nor in Jerusalem will you worship the Father. You worship what you do not know; we worship what we know, for salvation is from the Jews. But the hour is coming, and is now here, when the true worshipers will worship the Father in spirit and truth, for the Father is seeking such people to worship him. God is spirit, and those who worship him must worship in spirit and truth." The woman said to him, "I know that Messiah is coming (he who is called Christ). When he comes, he will tell us all things." Jesus said to her, "I who speak to you am he."

Just then his disciples came back. They marveled that he was talking with a woman, but no one said, "What do you seek?" or, "Why are you talking with her?" So the woman left her water jar and went away into town and said to the people, "Come, see a man who told me all that I ever did. Can this be the Christ?" They went out of the town and were coming to him.

Meanwhile the disciples were urging him, saying, "Rabbi, eat." But he said to them, "I have food to eat that you do not know about." So the disciples said to one another, "Has anyone brought him something to eat?" Jesus said to them, "My food is to do the will of him who sent me and to accomplish his work. Do you not say, 'There are yet four months, then comes the harvest'? Look, I tell you, lift up your eyes, and see that the fields are white for harvest. Already the one who reaps is receiving wages and gathering fruit for eternal life, so that sower and reaper may rejoice together. For here the saying holds true, 'One sows and another reaps.' I sent you to reap that for which you did not labor. Others have labored, and you have entered into their labor."

Many Samaritans from that town believed in him because of the woman's testimony, "He told me all that I ever did." So when the Samaritans came to him, they asked him to stay with them, and he stayed there two days. And many more believed because of his word. They said to the woman, "It is no longer because of what you said that we believe, for we have heard for ourselves, and we know that this is indeed the Savior of the world."

John 4:1–42

Who Was the Samaritan Woman?

While we don't know her name, we all know the "Samaritan woman" or "the woman at the well." Your first thought may have been: *The woman who had five husbands and was with yet another man.* Yup, that's her.

We've heard the sermons about Jesus seeking her out—going through Samaria when he didn't have to just so he could meet that woman. She wasn't the most influential woman in town. She probably wasn't the wealthiest or most spiritual. In fact, she was an outcast, a woman living a shameful life. Jesus offering her living water—salvation—is an encouragement for all of us. We might feel she didn't deserve his compassion and mercy, but the truth is, none of us do, which is why her story resonates with all who come to Christ. But maybe it resonates a little louder with those who have a few skeletons in their closets.

Much has been made about the time of day the woman came to the well to draw water. The Bible doesn't tell us the reason she was there later in the day. It seems she would have come early, before the heat of the day—before starting chores, cooking, or other things that would require water. Maybe, as is often suggested, she wanted to avoid the large group of women who would've been there in the early morning. The shame she carried would make the water jars even more unmanageable. It's a good possibility, and one we can easily relate to. Most of us avoid people and situations that cause discomfort. I think of the scene in *The Music Man* when all the women of the town pick a little, talk a little, cheep, cheep, cheep. Was she trying to avoid that scene?

Maybe she just had other commitments that morning or slept in. We just don't know. The important thing is that Jesus knew when she would be at the well and planned his day accordingly. It wasn't a chance encounter. Once again, Jesus surprised everyone with whom he chose to engage in conversation with, this time a Samaritan woman. And not just any conversation, but a conversation of eternal significance. If he was going to let the Samaritans in on his plan of salvation and the fact that he was the Messiah they were awaiting, why go to a woman? And why this woman? There must be a reason.

The Shame of Sexual Sin

The apostle Paul said that, "God chose what is foolish in the world to shame the wise; God chose what is weak in the world to shame the strong" (1 Corinthians 1:27). What could be more foolish and weak than a Samaritan woman who is an outcast, even among her own people? Certainly, Jesus wouldn't choose *her*, but he did, demonstrating the principle Paul taught. Jesus knew everything about her, and we can learn more about God's heart in this encounter.

Jesus starts the conversation simply enough, asking her for a drink of water. I imagine this woman looked around to see to whom he was speaking—it couldn't be her. But being the only one there, she engaged with him. She didn't just give him a drink and walk away. She recognized him as a Jew and knew that it was unusual for him to ask her for a drink. Jesus moved the conversation to the living water he can provide, heightening the difference between them, but also directing the conversation to true worship. Jesus was the master of moving a conversation from the mundane (a drink of water) to the eternal (living water).

But then he took their conversation to a more personal place. To get the explanation she desired, he told her to call her husband. Now, that hurt. She didn't have a husband, and he knew it and told her so. This is where we find God's heart for the sexually harmed or sexually broken. Jesus wasn't saying, "This is too important for a woman. Get your husband." He was intentionally exposing her shame in this area. She'd had five husbands and the man she was with now wasn't her husband. He was not exposing her sin to shame her, though. He was exposing her sin so that she could see her need—him, living water, salvation.

How did she lose five husbands? It couldn't have been easy. At that time, in that culture, a woman couldn't divorce her husband. Only a husband could initiate divorce. Did five men divorce her? Why? An acceptable reason to divorce a woman was infertility. Was she carrying the shame of infertility as well as multiple husbands? Each time she lost a husband, what happened to her? Did she find another as quickly as possible so that her needs would be met? Did any of these men love her? Were they good to her? Did she lose them to death? Imagine that pain, burying five husbands.

Or were these men taking advantage of her, knowing she couldn't survive on her own? Was this a form of trafficking? If the man she was currently with wasn't her husband, that would indicate a sexual relationship outside of marriage. At the very least, her reputation in town probably wasn't stellar. I think there was more to the conversation, since she tells people, "Come, see a man who told me *all that I ever did*" (v. 29, italics added for emphasis). I think Jesus shared some details that are left out of the story, probably details that answer some of my questions.

Chosen for Kingdom Work

But whatever the details, we have all we need to know. Jesus used this woman in all her sexual brokenness to reach the whole town with his message of salvation. That shows us something about God's heart for the sexually broken. He didn't have to do it this way. He chose to use her, maybe not in spite of her past, but because of it. As with anyone who turns to Jesus, her life was changed. I don't think she was the same woman after spending time with Jesus, and that would make an even bigger impact on those around her. He stayed in the town for a few days, teaching them and showing them he was the Messiah. We could look at the whole town as "less than" since they were half Jews, not full

Jews. And yet, Jesus went to them, they welcomed him, and the truth he shared with love and compassion won their hearts. And I bet the woman from the well had a front-row seat for all of it.

The change Jesus brings about in believers gives them courage to do hard things. If the speculation that the woman was at the well when no one else would be there is correct, imagine how hard it would've been for her to go into town and tell everyone about Jesus. She was compelled to do the very thing she was avoiding: engaging with the townspeople. But she couldn't keep the good news to herself, she had to testify about him. That testimony, though, was of exposed sin and shame. It's hard to share that kind of testimony.

For victims of sexual harm, sharing is also one of the first steps to healing. Shoving the trauma of sexual harm to the back of our mental and emotional closets will keep us stuck in it. It is when our past comes out of the darkness, into the light, that we can properly deal with it and move on from it. And that will take longer for some than others. Jesus showed his love for her by letting her share her testimony with the rest of the town, a necessary first step in healing.

Understanding Trauma

Trauma is different for everyone. It's not a one-size-fits-all kind of thing, and neither is recovery from it. We need to know that it's not the event that is traumatic, but how a person responds to the event. Two people who experience the exact same event, let's say an earthquake, will respond differently. For one it may be traumatic, but for the other it may be like any other event in their day.

My son lives in California. When I heard there was an earthquake in his area, I called and asked him about it. His response was, "I was in a parking lot and felt the shaking for a few seconds and thought, 'I think that was an earthquake.'" To him it was no big deal. But for someone who had experienced stronger quakes, or been hurt or lost a home or been involved in some sort of major event earlier in life, like a war or other violence, they may have reacted with terror.

Those differences happen because of what founder of Levanta La Voz (Raise Your Voice), Karen Shogren, describes as a trauma avalanche. A person who has experienced nonsexual abuse will develop traumatic responses like post-traumatic stress disorder. The longer it goes on, the more trauma they experience. A child who experiences trauma is more likely to react traumatically to future events. When sexual harm is added, the result can be severe trauma. Each event adds another layer of trauma, and, like an avalanche, it can come crashing down with one small shift or vibration. The woman at the well had layers of sexual experiences, so it would make sense that her trauma was layered as well. But Jesus had good news for her. No matter her past, there was a place for her in the kingdom of God.

Whether her sexual harm was her own doing or at the hands of the men in her life, she could be free from that past. As a believer in Jesus her Messiah, "There is therefore now no condemnation for those who are in Christ Jesus. For the law of the Spirit of life has set you free in Christ Jesus from the law of sin and death" (Romans 8:1–2). She also was no longer a slave to the effects of trauma.

Many people think they'll never be able to heal from the trauma of their past, but that is not true. Healing and freedom are found in Jesus. John 8:36 says, "If the Son sets you free, you will be free indeed." Nothing can keep a hold on you when you're in Jesus—not Satan, not sin, and not your past. And he not only offers freedom, but he also offers abundant life: "The thief comes only to steal and kill and destroy. I [Jesus] came that they may have life and have it abundantly" (John 10:10). This isn't financial abundance or some other form of prosperity. It is a fullness in life, a soul not stunted. And it's also a life of highs and lows, along with the ability to learn and grow through them.

Jesus Changes Everything

The Samaritan woman is a prime example of God's hand not being too short to save (see Isaiah 50:2). No one is too far gone or too sinful or too shameful for God to save. His grace extends to depths we can't even imagine because his love is just as great.

I often wonder what happened next. It's almost like the end of a book that you just know was a setup for the author's next book. You read that last page and can't wait for the next installment. Where did life take her? Did she remain with that man she was with? Did she find true love? Did she go on to do great things or live a quiet, content life?

Whatever came next, if her faith in Jesus was genuine, we know she was a new creature. The old had passed away. Jesus has that power, that living water, that doesn't just change us but satisfies us. There is no need to go anywhere else to be filled. It gives us power to turn from our past and the things that control us. And it sets us on a course of new life, new desires, and new goals. Not long after this event, after his death, burial, and resurrection, Jesus sent the Holy Spirit to continually work out the salvation of the believers, to help us keep growing in faith and obedience. This woman is someone I hope to meet in heaven one day, to sit down with and hear the rest of her story.

I think it will be like so many other women's stories I've known. A story of how Jesus took her shame and brokenness and turned them into a message of hope. And that hope was shared with others, when she offered them the living water that she had found, and they drank of it, and received hope. It kept on springing up, flowing from one broken vessel to another.

Jesus's offer of living water was a beautiful expression of grace. Grace is God's unmerited favor. There's nothing we can do to deserve it. He chooses to bestow it on whomever he wishes. His grace is life-changing, sufficient in all of our circumstances. Grace saves, justifies, gives endurance, allows us to live in fellowship with one another, and so much more.

What is God's heart for the Samaritan Woman?

Grace – Jesus offers this woman the gift of salvation through grace. His heart is grace—he is full of grace and truth (John 1:14). None of us deserve his grace, yet he offers it freely to all who believe in him.

* Ephesians 1:7 – "The riches of his grace" is a phrase worth pondering. What is the depth of the riches of his grace? What would that mean to those who struggle with sin?

* For the Samaritan woman and others who have a sinful past, it must be a relief to learn that salvation is not based on their works but entirely on grace. (See Ephesians 2:8–9.) Are you trying to earn salvation by works?

* God's grace breaks sin's hold over those who come to faith in him. (See Romans 6:14.) This woman experienced the freedom that comes through God's grace. What would you like to be free from?

* God's grace was extended to the whole community through the Samaritan woman's testimony. Has a testimony of God's grace in a difficult story spoken to you or sparked a community to turn to Christ?

* The Samaritan woman found new life and freedom from sin. This is what Jesus offers—an abundant life in him. John 10:10 says the thief comes to kill, steal, and destroy, but Jesus comes to give abundant life. What has the thief tried to steal or destroy in you and how has grace overcome it?

How can we apply the lessons from the Samaritan woman's story?

Effects of Trauma

* Think about what kinds of things add layers of trauma and what can set off the avalanche. Sexual trauma (whether it is from our own sin or someone harming us) can have severe consequences. Because we tend to hide sexual harm and sexual sin, it makes it even more difficult to overcome. But it is not impossible. The power of the Holy Spirit lives in the believer, and God has equipped Spirit-filled counselors who can help.

* The past is gone, and a new life is possible. Read 2 Corinthians 5:17; Galatians 2:20; and Colossians 3:3. The good news of the gospel, the living water Jesus offers, is that we can have a new life. Our old life, our past, with all of its sin and ugliness, is gone.

Shame and Guilt

* The Bible hints that the Samaritan woman's shame is why she went to the well later in the day. Shame is different than guilt. Guilt says we did something bad; shame says we are bad. Even though she tells the townspeople, "He told me all that I ever *did*," it's likely the Samaritan woman carried a lot of shame along with the guilt of what she did. Whatever the reason was for her having five husbands, at some point it would be logical that she saw herself as the problem. No matter what someone has done or what has been done to them, that is not who they are. They are children of God, made in his image, and we should do all we can to help them see themselves the way God sees them. He sees their need. He sees their worth. He sees a precious child.

* How has shame impacted your life?

* Shame is a liar that can keep you stuck in your past. Jesus said, "If you abide in my word, you are truly my disciples, and you will know the truth, and the truth will set you free" (John 8:31–32). Search his Word to find out who God says you are. Here are some verses to get you started: John 15:16; Romans 8:16, 37; and 2 Corinthians 5:21.

* If guilt is plaguing you because of sin—not false guilt because of shame—root it out of your life so that you can move forward. Pray through Psalm 32:1–5; 1 John 1:9; and Ephesians 2:1–10.

* The Samaritan woman overcame her shame and guilt to share Jesus with her community. God used her testimony to save many others. How can you share your story in the same way?

Chapter Eight
God's Heart of Gentleness:
The Woman Caught in Adultery – Living Victoriously

The Adulterous Woman's Story

John 8:1–11

> But Jesus went to the Mount of Olives. Early in the morning he came again to the temple. All the people came to him, and he sat down and taught them. The scribes and the Pharisees brought a woman who had been caught in adultery, and placing her in the midst they said to him, "Teacher, this woman has been caught in the act of adultery. Now in the Law, Moses commanded us to stone such women. So what do you say?" This they said to test him, that they might have some charge to bring against him. Jesus bent down and wrote with his finger on the ground. And as they continued to ask him, he stood up and said to them, "Let him who is without sin among you be the first to throw a stone at her." And once more he bent down and wrote on the ground. But when they heard it, they went away one by one, beginning with the older ones, and Jesus was left alone with the woman standing before him. Jesus stood up and said to her, "Woman, where are they? Has no one condemned you?" She said, "No one, Lord." And Jesus said, "Neither do I condemn you; go, and from now on sin no more."
>
> John 8:1–11

Who Was the Woman Caught in Adultery?

This story does not appear in some of the earliest manuscripts and most likely was not written by John. Because it is included in later manuscripts and is consistent with other interactions Jesus had, we're treating it as part of the canon of Scripture and an actual event in the life of Jesus on earth. In his article, "Does the Woman Caught in Adultery Belong in the Bible?" Tommy Wasserman, Professor of Biblical Studies at Ansgar Teologiske Høgskole in Kristiansand, Norway, concludes, "So, should the beloved story of the Woman Caught in Adultery be read in our churches? Yes, I think so. The story has the earmarks of a genuine gospel story albeit not original to John."[18]

Here we have a woman accused of adultery, reportedly caught in the act. We don't know whether this adultery had just happened, and she was dragged before Jesus directly from being caught, or if the adultery had happened some time before and she was just now being judged for it. Though the timing is not clear, the sin is clear. She was caught having sex with someone who was not her husband. The text tells us the reason for them bringing her to Jesus: to test him. It wasn't for righteousness's sake. It wasn't to purge sin from among them. It was to test Jesus. What would he say? Would he condemn this woman to death, as the Law required?

Perhaps the crowd expected Jesus to react with the same contempt for this woman that they did. They must have been very disappointed that he didn't jump up, condemn her, and pick up a stone. He would, after all, have been the only one able to stone her following his statement, "Let him who is without sin among you be the first to throw a stone at her" (John 8:7). It seems Jesus turned the test around on them. He would have been justified in stoning her. It was the Law. But his heart once again turned the Law on its head.

The scribes and Pharisees wanted to test him, to bring a charge against him. They were using this woman to that end. What charge were they trying to pin on Jesus? No matter, he didn't bite. Instead, he calmly but authoritatively diffused the situation by suggesting if there was a sinless man there, that he go ahead and throw the first stone. Their plan failed epically. The finger of accusation was pointing directly back at them. One by one, they dropped their stones and walked away.

As I picture this woman standing before Jesus, surrounded by an angry mob with stones ready to throw at her, I wonder what she was feeling. The obvious emotion would be fear. The fear of what was about to happen, her impending stoning and death. Fear is one of the most common feelings among abuse survivors—fear of their abuser, fear that someone will find out, fear that it was their fault, fear that it will happen again—so much fear. This woman must have been right at the edge of her greatest fears, but Jesus stepped in. My favorite phrase in the Bible is, "but God . . ." (For example, Psalm 73:26 says, "My flesh and my heart may fail, but God is the strength of my heart and my portion forever.") When God steps into our lives, everything changes. Even fears are stilled.

The woman stood there before him, the only one who could rightly accuse and judge her, and awaited her fate. Jesus asked her who had condemned her, and she answered, "'No one, Lord.' And Jesus said, 'Neither do I condemn you; go, and from now on sin no more'" (John 8:11). Her answer tells us that she recognized who he was—Lord, one with the authority to judge. But Jesus himself said he didn't come to condemn but to save. "For God did not send his Son into the world to condemn the world, but in order that the world might be saved through him" (John 3:17).

The Mercy and Gentleness of Jesus

As this scene transpired, did she realize that he wasn't just any judge but *the* judge? She knew she was guilty. She was caught in the act. But instead of judgment and condemnation, Jesus showed mercy, because that's the heart of God. He desires to show mercy. In *Gentle and Lowly: The Heart of Christ for Sinners and Sufferers*, pastor and author Dane Ortlund writes, "There is no love so great and so wonderful as that which is in the heart of Christ. He is the one that delights in mercy; he is ready to pity those that are in suffering and sorrowful circumstances; one that delights in the happiness of his creatures."[19]

His mercy was followed by an admonition: go and from now on sin no more. This interaction with Jesus shows us that when we are shown mercy, we are obligated to sin no more. Unlike most of the other women we've looked at, this woman chose to sin sexually. Her interaction with Jesus reveals a powerful truth: when Jesus enters your life, he gives you the power to choose not to sin. Before she met Jesus, she was a slave to sin, literally condemned to death. But after meeting Jesus and receiving mercy, she could become a slave to righteousness. She could choose to sin no more. What freedom that would have brought her.

But we don't know if she accepted his gift of mercy and actually turned from her sin. Maybe, like so many do, she rejected his offer of mercy and remained a slave to sin.

If she did accept Jesus's gift of mercy, she could walk away from her old life because it was dead, having no more power over her. Colossians 3 is one of my favorite passages. Verse 3 says, "For have died, and your life is hidden with Christ in God." Our former life, with all of its ugliness and sinfulness, is dead. It doesn't have any power over us anymore. It is "hidden with Christ."

Satan likes to throw it back in our faces, but we can remind ourselves that it is hidden with Christ. Our past, as well as our sin, was covered by the blood of Jesus on the cross. Our debt has been paid by Jesus. We don't owe it anymore. Anytime Satan or someone acting like the scribes and Pharisees in John 8 throw stones of accusation at us—you're not deserving of God's mercy, you're not really saved, you'll never be free from your past—we can stop them by reminding ourselves (and them, out loud if necessary) that our former self is dead and we are in Christ, no longer controlled by sin but by the Holy Spirit. And we can now live victoriously, able to sin no more and forgiven when we do sin and repent. I hope that is where this woman's story ended up, with her walking away in newness of life. He is a God of second chances. Although we don't know if she heeded his admonition, this story shows us his heart of mercy.

Jesus himself declared his intentions and purpose when he began his earthly ministry teaching in synagogues:

> And He came to Nazareth, where He had been brought up; and as was His custom, He entered the synagogue on the Sabbath, and stood up to read. And the book of the prophet Isaiah was handed to Him. And He opened the book and found the place where it was written,
>
> "The Spirit of the Lord is upon me, because he anointed me to preach the gospel to the poor.
>
> He has sent me to proclaim release to the captives, and recovery of sight to the blind, to set free those

> who are oppressed, to proclaim the favorable year of the LORD."
>
> Found in Isaiah 61:1-2

> And He closed the book, gave it back to the attendant and sat down; and the eyes of all in the synagogue were fixed on Him. And He began to say to them, "Today this Scripture has been fulfilled in your hearing."
>
> Luke 4:16-21 NASB 1995

Jesus was saying, "I am he. I am the one Isaiah wrote about." Jesus came to heal, to set captives free, to proclaim the good news of the gospel—that all who have faith in him will be saved. In this woman's story, he is living out what he proclaimed in that synagogue—setting her free from death, her oppressors, and the power of sin.

What About the Man Caught in Adultery?

It should be noted that there was no man involved in the adultery charges. The Law was that both caught in adultery should be stoned, not just the woman (see Leviticus 20:10). So where was the man? Why wasn't he accused of anything? There's lots of room for speculation here. Perhaps he had already been stoned or punished in some way. But since the Bible doesn't tell us any more about it, we'll leave it at that. This story is not telling us that men are not accountable. I would go so far as to say, in the Christian realm, men are even more accountable than women, since they are to be spiritual leaders and protectors. But they too can receive mercy.

Now, let's look at applying this point to today's world. All too often, women are accused of sexual sin, but not the man with whom they were sinning. There are countless stories of women losing jobs or positions because of an affair, while the man involved does not. Women are threatened and intimidated into silence when they're victims of sexual harassment. The "Me Too" movement opened the floodgates for women to take a stand and be heard.

Historically, women were expected to accept sexual harassment as part of the work environment. More and more women are now able to make accusations without fear of being fired or blacklisted, but there is still more work to be done. Again, God's heart for these women is that they would find justice. He will bring justice, if not in this life, in the one to come. Their abuses will not go unpunished; the guilty will pay a terrible price (see Psalm 110:5–6). But it's not always up to us to throw the first stone. We can leave that to the one who will take his own vengeance.

This point also reminds me of a story I learned about a girl who had been sexually abused by a man. They were in the same church, and the abuse was found out. As part of the church's discipline and restoration process, the two people had to stand before the church body and confess their sin. Yes, they both had to confess their part in the sin that took place. This was sin between an adult man and a minor child. She had no culpability in the sinful act, either legally or ethically. Yet, she was forced to stand before the church and confess. I can only imagine the shame that was wrongly heaped on her.

This is not the only story I've heard like this. In fact, more often than not victims are asked questions like ones I mentioned before, "What did you do to entice him? What were you wearing? Why were you there? Didn't you know better? What did you think would happen?" These kinds of questions are stones. When thrown, they bury a victim under more shame. Children are not responsible for the actions of an adult under any circumstances, and they deserve to be protected and cared for.

Instead of asking accusatory questions, as above, we can support victims with statements like, "It wasn't your fault. I'm glad you told me, and I will help you. You did the right thing in telling me. I'll be with you through whatever happens. I'm so sorry this happened to you." These are the kinds of responses that will make victims feel safe and free from shame. These are the kinds of responses Jesus would offer, so we should too.

Ministering to Survivors

Adult survivors of abuse often face the same types of questions. How can we minister to those in our midst who have survived sexual abuse or have walked away from sexual sin? Of course, sharing God's heart with them is of the utmost importance. They need to know that God rescued them because of his great love for them, that in him they are new creations, and their pasts are dead and hidden in Christ. He only sees them through the cleansing blood of Jesus, perfect and pure. His mercy and grace reach beyond anything that they did or was done to them. And we should tell them that God has given them gifts to be used to build his kingdom. He has created good works for them to do, just as he has done for all of his children.

As with the woman at the well, telling their story is the first step to healing. The church should be a place where we can share our stories, no matter how ugly. Every detail does not need to be shared for healing to take place. There should be discretion used depending on the audience. Not everyone is mature enough to hear the details of hard stories. They may react with some of the things in our "don't say" list. And others may be retraumatized by hearing a story similar to their own. It would be wise if every church had some women trained in ministering to survivors. What a blessing that would be for a survivor. Usually, survivors never share their stories or share them with unsafe people and end up more hurt and ashamed. When we consider that one in three women have been sexually abused, it indicates that there are a lot of hurting women in our congregations.

If you remember our brief discussion on trauma, apply it here. Not every survivor is the same. Some who have suffered abuse are not as traumatized as others. Some will need to share their story over and over; others will not want to share it at all. All will be dealing with some level of shame. Some may feel they're too broken to be used by God. We need to think through these issues and be ready when a survivor shares with us.

And remember that Jesus didn't condemn the woman in John 8. He showed her mercy. It is not our place to condemn those who have been sexually harmed or trapped in sexual sin. Rather, we need to model the love of God, be willing to listen to their stories, and walk with them as they work through their trauma.

What is God's heart for the Woman Caught in Adultery?

Gentleness – God is bent toward mercy, and his mercy showcases his gentleness. We all deserve his wrath, but he is gentle with us, knowing we are dust. Jesus demonstrates the gentleness of God in this encounter with the woman caught in adultery. What can we learn from his example—about God and about ourselves?

* God is gentle (Psalm 18:30–36; Matthew 11:29; Isaiah 40:11). Think about the different ways his gentleness is expressed in these verses. In what ways have you experienced his gentleness?

* We should imitate God's gentleness (Galatians 6:1; Philippians 4:5; Ephesians 4:2; 1 Peter 3:15–16). How can you show gentleness to those around you?

* Work on growing in gentleness (see Galatians 5:22–23; Colossians 3:12; James 3:17). Gentleness is required if we desire to accurately reflect Jesus to the world. Imagine you were present for the unfolding drama of the woman caught in adultery. How could you have shown gentleness to her? How can you show gentleness to those around you who are caught in sin right now?

* God's gentleness brings hope. The life of the woman caught in adultery was about to end. But Jesus's gentle answer brought her hope. Every survivor is looking for hope—hope of experiencing true freedom, hope for a good future, and hope that there is more to their life. God's Word and a relationship with Jesus are full of hope (see Romans 15:13; 2 Corinthians 1:9–10; 1 Peter 1:3). Do you have hope for your future?

How can we apply the lessons of the Woman Caught in Adultery?

Teach God's purpose for sex

* Satan distorts everything God created to be good, including sex. Discuss how can the church can teach about sex as something beautiful and created by God. This is countercultural (even in most church cultures).

* Teach parents and children what abuse is and how to talk about it.

* Be a safe person for the vulnerable to turn to and share their story.

Live victoriously

* We don't know how the woman in John 8 responded to the gentle mercy Jesus showed her. But it is a question we must all ask ourselves, as Pilate did in Matthew 27:22, "What shall I do with Jesus who is called Christ?" Will you answer like the crowd who yelled to crucify him, or will you accept his mercy and walk in newness of life, able to sin no more?

* Read 1 Corinthians 15:56–58; Genesis 4:7; 1 John 2:1–6; and 1 Corinthians 10:13–14. How can you live victoriously—fighting against sin, in the power of the Holy Spirit, knowing that Satan and sin are always tempting you but Jesus has overcome both so you can too?

* Think about your position in Christ: seated at the right hand of God, clothed in Jesus's righteousness, your past hidden with him. Thank God for his gentle mercy.

Chapter Nine
God's Heart of Forgiveness:
The Woman Who Crashed the Party – Humility

The Party Crasher's Story
Luke 7:36–50

One of the Pharisees asked [Jesus] to eat with him, and he went into the Pharisee's house and reclined at table. And behold, a woman of the city, who was a sinner, when she learned that he was reclining at table in the Pharisee's house, brought an alabaster flask of ointment, and standing behind him at his feet, weeping, she began to wet his feet with her tears and wiped them with the hair of her head and kissed his feet and anointed them with the ointment. Now when the Pharisee who had invited him saw this, he said to himself, "If this man were a prophet, he would have known who and what sort of woman this is who is touching him, for she is a sinner." And Jesus answering said to him, "Simon, I have something to say to you." And he answered, "Say it, Teacher."

"A certain moneylender had two debtors. One owed five hundred denarii, and the other fifty. When they could not pay, he cancelled the debt of both. Now which of them will love him more?" Simon answered, "The one, I suppose, for whom he cancelled the larger debt." And he said to him, "You have judged rightly." Then turning toward the woman he said to Simon, "Do you see this woman? I entered your house; you gave me no water for my feet, but she has wet my feet with her tears and wiped them with her hair. You gave me no kiss, but from the time I came in she has not ceased to kiss my feet. You did not anoint my head with oil, but she has anointed my feet with ointment.

> Therefore I tell you, her sins, which are many, are forgiven—for she loved much. But he who is forgiven little, loves little." And he said to her, "Your sins are forgiven." Then those who were at table with him began to say among themselves, "Who is this, who even forgives sins?" And he said to the woman, "Your faith has saved you; go in peace."
>
> Luke 7:36–50

Who Was the Woman Who Crashed the Party?

Jesus goes to lunch at the home of a Pharisee named Simon. We're not sure of the motive of this Pharisee. Perhaps, like so many others, he was trying to trap Jesus and bring a charge against him. Or maybe he knew inviting Jesus to his home would draw a crowd, giving this man his fifteen minutes of fame. Or maybe he really wanted to hear more from Jesus because he was close to believing that Jesus was the Christ. Whatever his motive, things didn't go exactly as planned when a sinful woman crashed the party.

She must have heard Jesus teaching before and believed his message. I'm sure she wasn't invited to the luncheon. She crashed it because she had to see Jesus. When she entered the scene, Jesus wasn't teaching; he was eating. She stood behind him, weeping, and noticed his feet were dirty. With love, respect, and kindness, she knelt at his feet, washed them with her tears, and anointed them with oil.

Of course, this act was noticed by the crowd, at least by the other two central figures, Jesus and Simon. The Pharisee, to his credit, didn't rebuke her publicly.

When Jesus asked him who loved more in the parable, Simon answered correctly. Did he have a big grin on his face? Most of us do when someone we want to impress says we did well. If he did, how quickly it must have faded when Jesus said that this sinful woman had treated him better than Simon had with the simple act of washing his feet. Ouch. Simon's smile was turned upside down.

Jesus Offers Peace

But then Jesus turned to the woman and told her, "Your sins are forgiven . . . Your faith has saved you; go in peace" (vv. 48, 50). The other guests were stunned. How could he forgive sins?

The woman knew. It was why she was there. The Son of God had drawn her there—to a place where even someone like her could find forgiveness and peace. Peace. Isn't that what all of us are really searching for? Someone like this woman, a sinful person (the wording indicates sexually sinful, possibly a prostitute) with no hope, could be forgiven and then promised peace. It almost seems too good to be true. Certainly, if we are trying to attain peace in this world, it is.

This world offers so many false avenues to peace: marriage, divorce, jobs, money, power, Botox, spirituality, and self-care. But none of them can lead to lasting peace because none of them can bring you peace with God. Only Jesus can do that. He is our conduit to peace with God. Until he is our peace, we are enemies of God. Jesus's death satisfied God's wrath and granted us peace. It's an incredible thing that ought to bring us to tears, as it did with this woman.

I wish we knew what had happened next. What was Simon's response? What about the other guests? What were the disciples thinking or saying? What was the rest of the lunchtime conversation like? I'm sure the writers, guided by the Holy Spirit, wrote what they felt was the most important information. As John puts it, the world could not contain the books that could be written about all Jesus said and did (John 21:25). It leaves us with so many questions, but we must trust that we were told all we needed to be told. (You may have noticed I remind myself of that often.)

Luke's gospel is written chronologically, unlike some of the others. While Luke doesn't tell us the rest of what happened that day, he does tell us where it led. The next chapter starts out, "Soon afterward he went on through cities and villages, proclaiming and bringing the good news of the kingdom of God. And the twelve were with him, and also some women who had been healed of evil spirits and infirmities" (Luke 8:1–2).

Here I go again with all my questions: Were others turning to Jesus because of what they saw or heard about at Simon's house that day? Was the sinful woman one of the women with him? We don't know where she ended up. All we know is that she led a sexually sinful life. We don't know how she got to that point. But she heard the good news of the gospel, she went to Jesus, he forgave her sin, and she went away in peace. Besides peace with God, she would also have peace from her past, peace for her present and future, peace that passes understanding, peace in her circumstances, and peace that grows as she follows Jesus.

That kind of peace is offered to all who trust in Jesus. I think there are two things survivors want more than anything else: hope and peace. They are not found in this world, despite all the world's promises. Promises are only as good as the person or entity making them. This world will fail us. For survivors of abuse, it has failed over and over again, which is why they lose hope. But God will never fail. His promises are sure because he cannot sin, and he cannot rescind what he has promised. It's not in his nature, not who he is, not his heart.

Jesus's forgiveness was soaked in love, mercy, and gentleness. Were her actions that day appropriate? Maybe not. Did Jesus chastise her for what she did? Did he say, "This is not the place or time"? No. He didn't condemn, because his heart is always bent toward mercy for his own. He did it out of love. He tells Simon that what she did to him was out of her love for him. He accepted her love and returned love by forgiving her and giving her peace. It's really a beautiful picture of how any of us come to Jesus. We come with all our failures and baggage. We don't clean ourselves up first, we just come as we are, and he does the work of making us new.

Sexual Sin Within the Church

Because this story happened in the home of a religious leader of the day, it lends itself well to a discussion on sin in the church, and the church's response to it. Have you heard of or read about a church leader failing in the area of sexual sin? I'm sure you have. Historically, the church has not been a leader in exposing the sins of sexual abuse in their midst. When a powerful church or ministry leader is found out, the crime is often unreported and swept under the rug. Many churches say that making it public would damage their reputation and the name of Jesus too much to risk it.

I think by now, we know that cover-ups only lead to more corruption and damage to the reputation of the universal church and the name of Jesus. Churches and church leaders need to care more about the well-being of the vulnerable among them than their own reputations. Sin and Satan have been defeated, but they are still trying to win. The best place for them to win is in the hearts of church leaders. If they get the leader, sin is mishandled, and the entire church could be destroyed. It might seem counterintuitive, but naming sin among us may be the best way to preserve the church's reputation.

Ephesians 5 is clear about this. Paul is talking specifically about sexual sin in the church when he writes this:

> Therefore be imitators of God, as beloved children. And walk in love, as Christ loved us and gave himself up for us, a fragrant offering and sacrifice to God.
>
> But sexual immorality and all impurity or covetousness must not even be named among you, as is proper among saints. Let there be no filthiness nor foolish talk nor crude joking, which are out of place, but instead let there be thanksgiving. For you may be sure of this, that everyone who is sexually immoral or impure, or who is covetous (that is, an idolater), has no inheritance in the kingdom of Christ and God. Let no one deceive you with empty words, for because of these things the wrath of God comes upon the sons of disobedience. Therefore do not become partners with them; for at one time you were darkness, but now you are light in the Lord. Walk as children of light (for the fruit of light is found in all that is good and right and true), and try to discern what is pleasing to the Lord. Take no part in the unfruitful works of darkness, but instead expose them. For it is shameful even to speak of the things that they do in secret. But when anything is exposed by the light, it becomes visible.
>
> vv. 1–13

Verse 11 in particular, "Take no part in the unfruitful works of darkness, but instead expose them," is a call to the church to expose sexual sin among themselves. By not exposing it, instead covering it up, the church is participating in the works of darkness. This is one way the church is seen as hypocritical by the world. We don't expose the sin in our own churches. It's also a major reason why so many young people walk away from church as they become adults. *Christianity Today* reported in 2019 that 32% of young adults stop attending church because they feel church members are judgmental or hypocritical.[20]

We can't say how much of that hypocrisy is related to sexual sin within the church. The secrecy involved and the underreporting of abuse make it difficult to gauge, but it is safe to assume that young adults have stopped attending church because of it.

Covering up sexual sin in the church also causes more harm to survivors. Most often, victims are not believed when they disclose abuse by a church leader. Typically, the church does its own investigation. It may even call for repentance and forgiveness, but it doesn't expose the sin or contact authorities. These actions, or nonactions, blame the victim and cause more hurt and shame. Victims are often cast as the sinners, the evildoers, the ones harming the church. We must ask ourselves if this is what Jesus would do. Based on this passage in Luke 7, and lots of other encounters Jesus had with both religious leaders and sinners, I'd have to say it is the exact opposite of what Jesus would do.

So what will we do? Let's not forget that everything should be done in love, but let's also get it right and show love to all involved. Love, and even forgiveness, does not mean there are no   consequences to sin. How should this play out? Should a pastor guilty of sexual abuse or misconduct be restored to his position? I think not. I think God's grace will cover his sin and restore him to faith and peace with God, but the consequences of his sin cannot be eliminated. I believe it is unwise to restore such men to places of authority in the church. It would be unloving to the victim to restore power to the offender. A truly repentant pastor would understand that and abide by the consequences of his actions and the discipline of the church.

In the early 2000s, C.J. Mahaney, formerly the president of Sovereign Grace Ministries (now Sovereign Grace Churches), covered up sexual abuse within the leadership of his church. Other church leaders stood behind him. After allegations came out and Pastor Mahaney and his church were under investigation in 2013, his supporters doubled down and had him as a keynote speaker at Together for the Gospel, a conference for pastors and church leaders. Albert Mohler, the well-respected president of Southern Baptist Theological Seminary in Kentucky, even joked about the allegations when he introduced Mahaney at the conference.

Mohler's words and attitude sent shock waves through the ranks of survivors of sexual abuse. They felt his handling of the situation was a kick in the gut, mocking their pain. One of them, Rachael Denhollander, the force behind the conviction of USA Gymnastics doctor Larry Nassar, asked to meet with him. After that meeting, a contrite Mohler made a statement that he hadn't realized the impact of his words on survivors and vowed to never behave that way again.[21]

Because there are so many Christians who have been harmed, it behooves church leaders to learn about the effects of abuse and care for their flock well. In doing that, they will care for all survivors well and just maybe turn the tide of the church into a place that shelters the broken. That would be where God's heart is. Psalm 34:18 says that God is near to the brokenhearted and saves those crushed in spirit. If we want to represent him well, we need leaders who will reflect God in this area.

The Church Attracts Abusers

One of the issues is that Christian organizations tend to be a magnet for abusers. It's easy to see why. The very nature of the church is to welcome in anyone, but especially those who need Jesus. We wouldn't be the church if we rejected outsiders or sinners or sufferers. We also tend to trust people quickly. If people are saying the right things, using "church" language, we don't question them. Every church seems to need help in the children's ministry. If someone comes to our church, saying the right things, acting the right way, we are quick to plug them into the children's ministry. Unfortunately, predators are exactly like the people I just described. They know the words, they know how to act, and they know we want to believe them.

I'm not suggesting we all become skeptics. Most people who work with children really do love children and have their best interests in mind. But we do need to be wary and have policies and protocols set up to keep our children as safe as possible. (Go to netgrace.org for resources and templates to create protection policies.)

Sometimes we do all we can, and still a child is molested, or an adult is sexually harmed within our church. What does that mean for them, for the church, and for the perpetrator? This is where the church needs to be the church. They need to love the victim, show compassion, and say the right things, not the wrong things. If a crime was committed (adult-on-child abuses are always a crime), we must contact the authorities. If it was an adult relationship, again we love the victim and give whatever help we can. We love the perpetrator by removing them from power and having them go through discipline, and we work toward restoring them to fellowship. Do not force the victim to offer forgiveness. Forgiveness may come over time, but it shouldn't be forced. We should offer outside-the-church counseling for all parties.

Sexual sin is a difficult thing for a church to go through and come out stronger than before, but it can be done. It's a living out of 2 Corinthians 1:3–10—comforting others as we have been comforted by God.

There are good examples of doing it right. One is found in Scot McKnight and Laura Barringer's *A Church Called TOV: Forming a Goodness Culture That Resists Abuses of Power and Promotes Healing*: "In our research, we learned of a compassionate, just, and truthful response to accusations of abuse at a Presbyterian church in Lexington, Kentucky. The church's senior pastor responded with such goodness and kindness and truth that I (Laura) was moved to tears reading his posts about his church's past and hopes for the future. He apologized publicly and specifically to victims, the Tates Creek congregation, and the entire community of Lexington."[22]

The church should be leading in this area, but we have been far behind the culture on the issue. It's time to step up and be the church, be Jesus, be God's heart for all involved. When we are, God will use these circumstances to create a beautiful message in the lives of survivors, perpetrators, and the church. And it will go a long way in showing God's heart of love, compassion, and mercy to a watching world.

What is God's heart for the Woman Who Crashed the Party?

Forgiveness – While we don't know this woman's name, we can relate to her. Even if our sin wasn't prostitution, all Christians come to Jesus broken and in need of his love and forgiveness.

* Psalm 32:1–5; Psalm 51; Psalm 103:12; Micah 7:19; Ephesians 1:7–8 – Our salvation, God's forgiveness of our sin, has no rival in our lives. God brings us from death to life and washes us clean, dressed in the beauty and righteousness of his Son, our relationship restored so we can spend eternity with him. What could compare? Nothing. And it is for all who would turn from sin and follow him. Salvation is for sinners—all sinners, no matter how despicable the sin. Have you asked

God to forgive your sins? Do you believe he has forgiven you and you are saved?

* In this story Jesus says, "Your sins are forgiven" (Luke 7:48). Do you understand that you have been transferred from the domain of darkness to the kingdom of light? Consider these passages: Colossians 1:12–14; Romans 8:1; and Psalm 103:10–13.

* Forgiveness brings peace. Jesus told the woman, "Your faith has saved you, go in peace" (Luke 7:50). Have you experienced the peace that comes from a restored relationship with God? (See Romans 5:1; John 16:33; Romans 15:13.)

* Read Romans 10:13–17. This is an interesting connection. How could you apply the beautiful feet in Romans to Jesus's feet in our story?

How can we apply the lessons of the Woman Who Crashed the Party?

Humility

What we see in this story is a sinful woman who genuinely wants to change and a church leader whose pride is exposed. It is a reminder that our churches are filled with sinners in need of our love and acceptance, which doesn't negate our responsibility to expose the sin in our midst. In short, we are all in need of humility because either of them could be us.

* Welcome sinners and survivors into the church family, remembering, "Your faith has saved you." And now what? They become part of the body. They need to learn and grow, discover their gifts so that they can serve, and give and receive the love of a body of believers. When one part hurts, all parts hurt. Give more honor to the weaker parts and consider others more important than yourselves (Romans 12; 1 Corinthians 12:12–26).

* Be aware that churches are magnets for abuse. Have policies and procedures in place to do all you can to keep predators out. Understand that predators appear like everyone else; there are few warning

signs. Part of their persona is that you trust them. Brainstorm some ways you can make your church as safe as possible.

* Expose sexual misconduct within the church, and don't just expose it but offer help. There are two mistakes churches tend to make: ignoring sexual misconduct and failing to protect victims. Once an incident is known, how can you/your church best address it, the victim, and the perpetrator? (Notify authorities, tell your congregation—without names if possible, remove the perpetrator from any ministry/leadership position, meet the victim's needs—counseling, being present, listening to them, offering help/prayer, going with them during the legal process, etc.)

Consider this from Mary DeMuth: "Secrets fester and ruin the lives of the silent. Secrets are powerful and pervasive. They thrive in shame-based systems where perfection is heralded and sin and weakness are covered up. Secrets don't last long in authentic, safe communities, but they multiply in systems—churches, sports teams, families, schools—where reputation matters more than safety."[23]

Chapter Ten

This I Know, That God Is for Me

A Look at Psalm 56

As we come to the end of this study on God's heart for the sexually harmed, my prayer is that you have found out that he is *for* you. The harm you suffered was not accidental or outside of his control or his love. It was part of his good plan for you, in part so that you can know him more deeply. Plumbing the depths of God's heart comes through suffering. Instead of wondering "*Why me?*" can you be thankful that he entrusted a time of suffering to you so that you can know him more deeply and experience his love in a way that is not possible without suffering?

Recently, during a discussion on suffering, a woman said, "I've been blessed. I really haven't experienced much suffering in my life." My immediate thought was, *Hmm, I wouldn't call that blessed. Suffering is what drew me to Jesus. Suffering is where I learned purpose and ministry in comforting others. Suffering is where I experienced God's heart of love, grace, compassion, justice, and restoration in a measure not possible in a life devoid of suffering. I am blessed for having suffered much.*

But I didn't say it out loud. Some people think I'm just giving a trite answer—what I'm supposed to say about suffering, making it sound good. It's not a trite answer; it's something my heart has wrestled with and honed over many, many years. And it hasn't been easy or simple. When suffering strikes now, though, it is my immediate response to ask God what he wants to teach me. I get a little excited, knowing that all suffering has purpose, and that God has something else for me to learn and share with others, but especially that he will show me more of the depths of his heart. Everything we suffer is because God is for us.

Where does the phrase, "God is for me," come from? Psalm 56. When I was struggling to come up with a title for this book, I read this psalm.

Then I got to verses 9–11 and read:

> "Then my enemies will turn back
>
> in the day when I call.
>
> This I know, that God is for me.
>
> In God, whose word I praise,
>
> in the LORD, whose word I praise,
>
> in God I trust; I shall not be afraid. What can man do to me?"

I knew I had found what I wanted to convey to my fellow sufferers. Let's take a look at the whole psalm, applying it to the common thoughts and feelings of those who have been sexually harmed:

> Be gracious to me, O God, for man tramples on me;
>> all day long an attacker oppresses me;
>
> my enemies trample on me all day long,
>> for many attack me proudly.
>
> When I am afraid,
>> I put my trust in you.
>
> In God, whose word I praise,
>> in God I trust; I shall not be afraid.
>
>> What can flesh do to me?
>
> All day long they injure my cause;
>> all their thoughts are against me for evil.
>
> They stir up strife, they lurk;
>> they watch my steps,
>>
>> as they have waited for my life.
>
> For their crime will they escape?

In wrath cast down the peoples, O God!

You have kept count of my tossings;

> put my tears in your bottle.

> Are they not in your book?

Then my enemies will turn back

> in the day when I call.

> This I know, that God is for me.

In God, whose word I praise,

> in the LORD, whose word I praise,

in God I trust; I shall not be afraid.

> What can man do to me?

I must perform my vows to you, O God;

> I will render thank offerings to you.

For you have delivered my soul from death,

> yes, my feet from falling,

that I may walk before God

> in the light of life.

vv. 1–13

First, we need context, even when applying it personally. It's a psalm of David from when the Philistines seized him in Gath. He was under attack and running for his life.

Feeling Trampled?

Verses 1 and 2 tell us about the ones trying to harm him and start with him calling on God's graciousness. His words could certainly be the words of someone who is being or has been sexually harmed, almost literally the experience of many: "Be gracious to me, O God, for man tramples on me; all day long an attacker oppresses me; my enemies trample on me all day long, for many attack me proudly."

From my many conversations with abuse survivors over the past thirty years, I have heard words so similar to these, it's eerie. They may not have used the word *trample*, but it perfectly describes how they felt—trampled underfoot, abused, molested, not cared about, squashed. And then David says that many attack him proudly. That perfectly describes a sexual predator, especially of children. They are proud. They think they cannot be caught. They abuse boldly, sometimes in public or in front of parents, which convinces the child that no one cares. It is all part of the grooming process and the pride of the perpetrator. They will take more risks as time goes by, leading to more pride in not getting caught. It also leads to more despair for the victim, who believes no one will come to their aid.

Trust in God

But God (remember, my favorite phrase) will rescue them. Verse 3 should be a memory verse for everyone: "When I am afraid, I put my trust in you." No matter what, I know I can trust God. Fear often rules victims and survivors, but God can overcome our fears. Couple that with the next few verses:

> In God, whose word I praise,
>> in God I trust; I shall not be afraid.
>
> What can flesh do to me?
>
> All day long they injure my cause;
>> all their thoughts are against me for evil.
>
> They stir up strife, they lurk;
>> they watch my steps,
>> as they have waited for my life.
>
> For their crime will they escape?
>> In wrath cast down the peoples, O God!
>
> vv. 4–7

Doesn't this sound just like those who abuse? They frighten, they injure, their thoughts are evil, they stir up strife, they lurk, they watch my steps, they wait to take my life. It's the grooming process in a nutshell. I'm especially caught by the phrase, "They have waited for my life." Sexual predators are patient. They allow their grooming process to dictate how long to wait before molestation or rape actually happens. By then, the victim is usually too ashamed or brainwashed to see a way out.

This I Know, That God Is For Me

But David gives us good news. Will they escape their crime? Maybe in this life they will, but God will not let their sins go unpunished. At some point, the wrath of God will come down on them. Unless, of course, they turn to Jesus, who took that wrath for them. In either case, justice will be done. Peter speaks to this in his second letter:

> "For if God did not spare angels when they sinned, but cast them into hell and committed them to chains of gloomy darkness to be kept until the judgment; . . . if by turning the cities of Sodom and Gomorrah to ashes he condemned them to extinction, making them an example of what is going to happen to the ungodly; and if he rescued righteous Lot, greatly distressed by the sensual conduct of the wicked (for as that righteous man lived among them day after day, he was tormenting his righteous soul over their lawless deeds that he saw and heard); then the Lord knows how to rescue the godly from trials, and to keep the unrighteous under punishment until the day of judgment, and especially those who indulge in the lust of defiling passion and despise authority."
>
> 2 Peter 2:4, 6–10

The next set of verses from Psalm 56 are particularly precious in my relationship with God:

> You have kept count of my tossings;
>
> > put my tears in your bottle.

> Are they not in your book?
>
> Then my enemies will turn back
>
> > in the day when I call.
>
> This I know, that God is for me.
>
> In God, whose word I praise,
>
> > in the LORD, whose word I praise,
>
> in God I trust; I shall not be afraid.
>
> What can man do to me?
>
> vv. 8-11

Psalms are songs meant to be sung. These verses seem to flow in a musical progression just waiting to burst into a song. My soul wants to sing them out in a chorus of praise. How near and personal and caring is God who keeps count of my sleepless nights, tossing and turning because of the anguish I am experiencing. He doesn't ignore my tears. He doesn't tell me to stop crying. He keeps my tears in his bottle and writes them in his book because they are precious and meaningful to him. I think when we are finally in the new heaven and God wipes away our tears, these are the ones the Bible is referring to. He'll empty the bottle and tear the pages from his book. Never will tears be a part of our life again.

As a sidebar, I think often about the imagery of God's bottle of tears. I think of it as one bottle with everyone's tears, not individual bottles. I don't know if that's true, but that's how I see it in my mind. If there is only one bottle with all the tears of his children, then the tears that Jesus shed while living as a man are in there as well. My tears and your tears, mixing with Jesus's tears. Something about that warms my spirit.

No Fear – What Can Man Do To Me?

Two of the sentences in the last section go together: "Then my enemies will turn back in the day when I call ... What can man do to me?" (vv. 9, 11).

For those of us who have suffered great things, we know what man can do. But what can he really do? He can't take my spirit. Even if he takes my life, all that does is free my spirit. And, again, God will deal with him. He will want to turn and run, but he can't run from God's judgment.

And finally, we come to the title of this book: "This I know, that God is for me" (v. 9). David offers praise to God and his word and confesses his trust in God, which brings him to say, "I shall not be afraid" (v. 11). God can work amazing things in us when we trust him. Remember, his heart is bent toward mercy. It is bent toward us. His heart is for us. He is not just *for* us; he is *against our enemies*. We need not be afraid; he is on our side. Everything he brings into our lives will be for our good, even when it seems our enemies will overtake us.

Give Thanks to God!

> The psalm concludes with verses 12–13:
> I must perform my vows to you, O God;
> > I will render thank offerings to you.
> For you have delivered my soul from death,
> > yes, my feet from falling,
> that I may walk before God
> > in the light of life."
>
> vv. 12–13

No matter the circumstances of my life, I will be faithful to God because he is faithful to me. His faithfulness never fails, even when mine does. I will thank him in my suffering, making it a sweet offering to him, and he will teach me through it. If you think that God didn't rescue you, that he didn't keep you from falling, realize that because you're still alive, he has rescued you. And he has a work for you to do, walking before him in the light of life.

We used Ephesians 5:1–13 several times throughout this book. It's all about being the light of Christ that exposes the darkness. Darkness cannot remain when light is present. You carry that light if you are in Christ, able to walk in love as Christ loved and exposing the deeds of darkness. You can light the way that is good and right and true for those still in darkness.

Take time to meditate on Psalm 56, and I encourage you to study Ephesians 5:1–13 some more, asking God how you can make a difference to those still in darkness. Psalm 73 is another psalm to meditate on. I want to share just the last two verses because they so perfectly sum up this chapter and God's justice for those who harm and his heart for those harmed:

> For behold, those who are far off from you shall perish;
>
> you put an end to everyone who is unfaithful to you.
>
> But for me it is good to be near God;
>
> I have made the Lord GOD my refuge,
>
> that I may tell of all your works."
>
> Psalm 73:27–28

Leader Notes

Chapter 1

They are listed as heroes of faith, what does that teach us about God's heart?

(Read Hebrews 11:8–12.)

God's forgiveness extends to perpetrators of abuse, as it did to Abraham and Sarah. In this story, Abram and Sarai failed, but their faith would grow, and they would be commended for their faith. Perhaps this failure was a step in that growth of faith. Sometimes we need our sin to be right in our face before we turn from it and move toward righteousness—repentance, forgiveness, growth, and maturity.

There is no sin that God cannot forgive, except the sin of unbelief.

Who can bring a charge against God's elect? It is God who justifies. Nothing can separate us from the love of God. (Look at Romans 8:31–39 and discuss God's love vs. our sin.)

Why can we trust God's faithfulness? God's promises are not dependent on who he makes the promises to—sinful people. God's promises are sure and trustworthy because he is the one who made them, and he is always faithful.

Chapter 2

God's heart of kindness, faithfulness, and redemption is beautifully summed up in Isaiah 63:7 – 9:

> I will recount the steadfast love of the LORD,
>
> the praises of the LORD,

according to all that the LORD has granted us,

    and the great goodness to the house of Israel,

that he has granted them according to his compassion,

    according to the abundance of his steadfast love.

For he said, "Surely they are my people,

    children who will not deal falsely."

And he became their Savior.

In all their affliction he was afflicted,

    and the angel of his presence saved them;

in his love and in his pity he redeemed them;

    he lifted them up and carried them all the days of old.

Isaiah 63:7–9

These verses from Isaiah 63 talk about God's heart for his people, specifically ancient Israel. It's easy to relate the words to those who have suffered harm as well. His heart doesn't change. He still desires to show kindness and faithfulness and be a Savior to his people. Verse 9 speaks directly to the question of where he was in our affliction—he was there, afflicted with us and saving us, even if we weren't immediately rescued. Because we are survivors, he did save us. And out of his compassion, he brings healing, continuing to save us.

Chapter 3

How did Israel's culture get to this point? How did God show justice and mercy?

(Read Judges 20:24–28, 35.)

Judges not only includes the disturbing story of sexual abuse to the Levite's concubine, but it also contains one of the most disturbing verses in the Bible, one that should serve as a warning for all of us. That verse is Judges 2:10, following the death of Joshua, it says, "And all that generation also were gathered to their fathers. And there arose another generation after them who did not know the LORD or the work that he had done for Israel." How did this generation, who saw their fathers die in the wilderness because of their disobedience, but also saw God part the Red Sea; collapse the walls of Jericho; and so many other miraculous moments of provision, not tell their children who God was or the things he had done? That is the answer to the question, "How did Israel's culture get to this point?" They had forgotten God and didn't tell their children all he had done. So, just two generations post-exodus, Israel did not know the LORD or the work he had done for Israel.

But God showed his justice and mercy in this story. Unfortunately, his justice meant that many Israelites had to die. But in his mercy, he used the deaths of one woman and thousands of men to turn his people back to him.

How can we shift the culture to see sexual sin as wicked, etc.? Take a stand for right and wrong. Call sin sin, even within the church. Expose evil—flood darkness with light (Ephesians 5).

How should the church (we) respond when we learn of sexual harm in our communities or congregations? Report it to proper civil authorities if a crime was committed (adults abusing children is always a crime); don't hide it, ignore it, or sweep it under the rug; be transparent with the community/congregation; and care properly for the victims and perpetrators.

For other places our children are involved, such as school, sports, scouts, etc., we need to be vocal, asking about the group's child protection policies. This alone will warn predators that we are watching, and they will likely leave our children alone, and maybe protect all the children connected to ours (i.e. team members and classmates).

Chapter 4

Telling victims the sexual harm was not their fault is especially important when the perpetrator is someone no one would expect could harm another, like when the perpetrator is their own husband. It's difficult to prove rape or sexual assault when it happens in a marriage relationship. Like the things discussed in the story of David and Bathsheba, we need to understand the context of what happened, and that sexual harm does, indeed, happen within marriage relationships. And it's not the victim's fault. In these cases, it is imperative that we do all we can to make sure the victim is in a safe place and has the support needed.

Chapter 5

How can we help survivors restore their voice, power, and relationships? Give them an opportunity to share their story, listen to and believe them, allow them to grieve what was lost, and walk alongside them, reminding them often of God's love and acceptance.

Churches could have laywomen trained in walking alongside those who have experienced sexual harm, knowing what to say and what not to say, offering appropriate resources, or just being a listening ear.

Chapter 6

Most of the notes for chapter six are at the end of that chapter because I felt the topics discussed there were the most difficult and important. I didn't want to push the notes on them to the back of the book, so included here is a more in-depth look at Psalm 22.

What does Psalm 22 teach us about the question, "Where was God?" Jesus cried out on the cross, "My God, my God, why have you forsaken me?" He was quoting the beginning of Psalm 22. Had God forsaken him? Had he turned his face from him? Did sin separate Jesus from his Father? No. The triune God cannot be separated. God the Father never took his eyes off his Son, just as he never takes his eyes off us, even when we sin. I think what Jesus was doing on the cross, weak as he was in his human body, was reciting Psalm 22—maybe for his own benefit or maybe for those watching, including his mother, his disciples, and even the religious leaders who had plotted to kill him. They likely would have known the psalm, a psalm of David. Jesus started reciting it, and when perhaps too weak to continue, did the rest of the psalm come to their minds? And as they watched his crucifixion, did the psalm keep coming to their minds? Suppose when he started the first lines of the psalm, those who were watching remembered the next seven verses:

> My God, my God, why have you forsaken me?
>> Why are you so far from saving me, from the words of my groaning?
> O my God, I cry by day, but you do not answer,
>> and by night, but I find no rest.
> Yet you are holy,
>> enthroned on the praises of Israel.
> In you our fathers trusted;
>> they trusted, and you delivered them.
> To you they cried and were rescued;
>> in you they trusted and were not put to shame.
> But I am a worm and not a man,
>> scorned by mankind and despised by the people.
> All who see me mock me;
>> they make mouths at me; they wag their heads;
> "He trusts in the LORD; let him deliver him;
>> let him rescue him, for he delights in him!"
>
>> (vv. 1–8)

And as the events of the crucifixion played out, perhaps more of the psalm was recalled:

> I am poured out like water,
>> and all my bones are out of joint;
> my heart is like wax;
>> it is melted within my breast;
> my strength is dried up like a potsherd,
>> and my tongue sticks to my jaws;

> you lay me in the dust of death.
>
> For dogs encompass me;
>
> > a company of evildoers encircles me;
>
> they have pierced my hands and feet—
>
> I can count all my bones—
>
> they stare and gloat over me;
>
> they divide my garments among them,
>
> > and for my clothing they cast lots.
>
> (vv. 14–18)

The most significant thing about the psalm is verse 24:

> For he has not despised or abhorred
>
> > the affliction of the afflicted,
>
> and he has not hidden his face from him,
>
> > but has heard, when he cried to him.
>
> (v. 24)

So, while the psalmist started out by asking God why he had forsaken him, he ended the psalm assured that God had not hidden his face from him; rather, God heard him when he cried. Verse 21 says that God rescued him. If Jesus thought that God had forsaken him, would he then have said, "Father, into your hands I commit my spirit!" (Luke 23:46) as he breathed his last? Perhaps Jesus was reminding those watching his crucifixion that God will never forsake them, no matter how ugly, sinful, or difficult their suffering. Do you think God turned away from Jesus? Do you think he turned away from you? Why or why not?

Chapter 7

How do shame and guilt affect a survivor of sexual harm?

Search the Scriptures to find out who you are in Christ. Start with these passages: 2 Corinthians 5:17 (a new creation), John 15:16 (chosen), Romans 8:16 (a child of God), Romans 8:37 (a conqueror through his love), Galatians 2:20 (loved), and 2 Corinthians 5:21 (given the righteousness of Christ).

Chapter 8

God is gentle (Galatians 6:1; Psalm 18:30–36; Matthew 11:28–30)

The idea that Jesus and God the Father describe themselves as gentle may be one of the most important attributes a survivor will learn about God's heart. Gentleness is not typically part of a survivor's world. Psalm 18 is a powerfully written psalm using strong military language. Look at verses 6–15, where David calls on God in his distress, and note the intensity of how God showed up. In verse 35, David says it is God's gentleness that made him great. Then David says he beats his enemies into dust and sweeps them away. David goes on to talk about God rescuing him, executing vengeance for him, delivering him, and subduing his enemies. I think this psalm is a good study for survivors because it shows God rescuing his child in dramatic ways, but everything seems to hinge on his gentleness—a picture of his heart for his children. Where have you seen the gentleness of God?

God brings hope. The life of the woman caught in adultery was about to end. She had to have felt that. Everyone around held stones, aimed at her. She waited to feel the blows, but Jesus de-escalated the situation. One by one each stone fell harmlessly to the ground. He spoke gently to her. Her accusers were gone. Her life was spared. A new life awaited her. She had hope. Every survivor is looking for hope—hope of experiencing true freedom, hope for a good future, hope there is more to their life—and God's Word and a relationship with Jesus are full of hope (see Romans 15:13; 2 Corinthians 1:9–10; 1 Peter 1:3). Do you have hope for your future?

Chapter 9

Forgiveness

In Luke 7:48, Jesus says, "Your sins are forgiven." **Do you understand that you have been transferred from the domain of darkness to the kingdom of light?** Like this sinful woman, no matter what your story, the forgiveness that Jesus offers obliterates your past. Meditate on that and consider these passages: Colossians 1:12–14; Romans 8:1; and Psalm 103:10–13.

Peace: In John 14:27, Jesus says, "Peace I give to you. Not as the world gives do I give to you." **How does the world try to give peace? What is the difference between the world's peace and the peace that Jesus offers?**

Love, compassion, gratefulness, and acceptance: Read Philippians 3:8–10. **How would it apply to this story?** (The woman gave something costly, oil in an alabaster jar. Simon, the Pharisee, saw her through the view of his own righteousness). Read Romans 10:13–17. How could you apply the beautiful feet in Romans to Jesus's feet in our story?

Jesus's feet are an important part of the story. Simon is rebuked for not washing them. The woman is commended for washing them with her tears. They both needed to hear the gospel brought by his beautiful feet.

Bonus Chapter

My Story

The Bible doesn't give us a script for forgiveness in any of the stories we studied. The closest would be David and Bathsheba because we have Psalm 51. But we don't know what he said to *her*—did he sing her the song of repentance he wrote? And what was their relationship like after that? We have to pull from other biblical accounts and passages to see how to forgive and what forgiveness looks like for survivors. I'm inviting you into my story of sexual abuse so you can see how forgiveness was worked out in the story of one survivor.

My Story

Throughout this book, I have mentioned pieces of my story. Here is the whole thing in a nutshell (the unabridged version is in my book, *Hidden With Christ: Breaking Free from the Grip of Your Past*). I was molested by a family friend from the time I was five or six years old until I was fifteen. It ended abruptly when my sister's boyfriend confronted my abuser. For the first time, I had hope and protection but also a tremendous amount of fear, shame, and despair. A year later, I was born again and truly felt like a new person. I put all of my past behind me, never to be heard from again. But God had other plans.

Ten years later, my abuser was arrested in another case, and I told the police my story. They wanted to use me as a witness to show that this man had a long history of abuse. My story became public, something I never wanted. But God has used it in ways I never would have dreamed. I saw that my abuse was something he had entrusted to me to help others. Over time, I became thankful that God was using my past sufferings because helping others through the healing process was such a blessing to me. So, how did I get where I am today—free from the past, living the abundant life Jesus promises in John 10:10?

Just before my abuser was arrested, I realized I was harboring a lot of resentment toward him. Not just because of what he had done to me, either. By the time of his criminal case, dozens of women had come forward but only two were considered "worthy" of witnessing. The others' lives were plagued with issues that would not make them good witnesses. I was sure that the shambles of their lives were because of what they had suffered, and it irked me. Following his conviction, he was sentenced to four years in jail but only served two months before he was released. He went back to his life as if nothing had happened. My resentment returned with a vengeance—and vengeance was exactly what I wanted—to the extent that I didn't want him to be saved because then he wouldn't have to pay for his sins.

The Beginning of Forgiveness

But God started working on my heart in new ways. I thought I had forgiven my abuser because he didn't take up much space in my head. I never thought about him. I considered my indifference toward him to be forgiveness. It wasn't. It was the natural result of time and distance. But the year I spent waiting for his trial revealed to me that I had work to do to forgive him.

The work of forgiveness started vertically. First, I asked God to forgive my resentment of him and any bitterness that was in my heart toward him, at my mother for not believing me when I told her about it, and anything else that was keeping me stuck spiritually. I had to deal with my own sin first.

As Christians, we don't have the option of refusing to forgive. We forgive because God has forgiven us. Jesus told the parable of the unforgiving servant in Matthew 18:21–35 to emphasize that our sin against God was much bigger than any sin someone could commit against us, yet he freely forgives. Jesus taking the debt of our sin on himself on the cross is the ultimate act of forgiveness. When we forgive someone, we absorb their debt to us. That may cost us something, which is why we need to work on it. But when we tell someone they are forgiven, that debt is gone. We cannot keep collecting on it or expect the person to pay on it if it doesn't exist. Any time a past hurt comes up, we must remind ourselves that it was forgiven and move on from it. With time and healing, it will become easier, and we will genuinely be free of any malice when we think of the person who harmed us.

I didn't realize that working on forgiving was really working on healing. I was just being obedient to God's command to forgive those who have wronged me. My motivation was to have a forgiving heart and therefore being in right standing with God. Too often I see forgiveness from selfish motives. I call it Facebook Theology. It's based on a popular meme that says forgiveness is not meant to set the perpetrator free, it's to set me free. That's not biblical forgiveness at all. Forgiveness is all about freeing the sinner from their debt. There will be personal benefits from forgiving someone, but they shouldn't be our motivation. And God cares about our motives in all we do, including forgiveness.

The Beauty of Reconciliation

It is a very special thing for a survivor to forgive horizontally—person-to-person—with a genuinely repentant offender. I met a woman who was able to not only forgive her father for abusing her as a child, but was also able to reconcile with him. They had a beautiful relationship in his later years. Our God is in the business of reconciliation. Jesus died to reconcile us to the Father. And if it is safe to do so, reconciliation would be an amazing testimony of God's work in both lives.

It was not possible in my case. My abuser never admitted his wrongdoing and never asked for forgiveness and has since died. Although reconciliation was not possible, that doesn't mean I can't forgive. I believe my heart is in a state of forgiveness toward him, which is evidenced by my concern for his soul when I heard that he had died, instead of being happy about it—which would have been my reaction had he died years ago.

Forgiveness Does Not Mean You Should Continue in a Harmful Relationship

One of the things I learned was that forgiveness doesn't mean remaining in or putting ourselves in a situation where we may be harmed again. My abuser was a school bus driver. In my senior year of high school, he was driving the late bus for kids who had after-school activities. I was terrified when I saw him but thought it would be okay with all the other kids on the bus, and I should have been the first stop. But he changed his route, making me the last drop-off. Alone on the bus, I sat all the way in the back. He taunted me, telling me what he was going to do to me when I came close to him to exit the bus.

But God intervened, providing a neighbor outside as the bus pulled up to my house. He was a fellow bus driver and started talking to my bus driver, giving me the opportunity I needed to scamper out the door without him having the ability to touch me. I was very careful after that to stay far away from him.

I have spoken to so many women who felt that if they had truly forgiven the man who harmed them, they should be able to remain in a relationship with them. Most often it was a family member. The abusers will even use this as a tactic to gaslight a victim into remaining with them. Putting yourself in a potentially harmful situation is not related to forgiveness. Forgiveness requires repentance. If someone is using forgiveness as a means to keep a person in a harmful situation, they are not repentant. And it is not wise to stay with them.

Forgiveness does not erase consequences. The perpetrator may need to go to jail, separate from you, or have supervised visits. Those are consequences of his sin that have nothing to do with unforgiveness.

God Never Needs to Be Forgiven

I have been asked many times if I was angry with God. It was never part of my story, but I have met numerous women who were. That is something to work on in the healing process, but God is never in need of forgiveness. We may not understand his ways or why he would use man's sinfulness to accomplish his purposes, but he never sins (see James 1:13). Therefore, he never needs to be forgiven. I mention this because it has become a popular idea, espoused by a few best-selling authors, but it is a dangerous false teaching.

Forgiveness Accomplished

My story became public just over thirty-five years ago. I have been working on healing ever since. I found that forgiveness was a choice I made every time something about my abuser came up. Today I can truly say that I don't hold any debt against him. My desire for vengeance is gone, but I also know that God will be perfectly just concerning him. Perhaps he repented and is in heaven. I would be truly happy to see him there.

For more reading on forgiveness for survivors, I highly recommend Dr. Bryan Maier's book, *Forgiveness and Justice: A Christian Approach*. And for more study from Scripture: Luke 17:3–4; Mark 11:25; Colossians 3:13; Romans 12:17–21; Colossians 2:13–14; and Romans 4:7–8.

Acknowledgments

I wrote this book because so many survivors tell me they don't think the Bible addresses sexual harm. Or that God doesn't care about victims and survivors. Or that God can't use them because of their past. I hope, through this study, you have found that the Bible does address sexual harm and God's heart for those who suffer. I also hope you see that God has used victims of sexual harm in the past, and he will use you too.

Many thanks to my dear friend, Karen Shogren: thanks for your encouragement to write this book, thanks for your contributions in content and allowing me to share it, thanks for your friendship and making me laugh in tough times, and thanks especially for answering God's call to minister to survivors and the church.

I'd like to thank my pastor, David Matchette, for his encouragement, prayers, and red pen—all of which were greatly appreciated. And thank you to two special pastors in my life who were so willing to answer my questions or just have a conversation about anything from the original Hebrew to proper application: my son, Reverend Timothy Radcliff, and my friend, Dr. Gary Shogren.

Thank you to the group of women who participated in the cohort of this book to check the content and viability of this study. Your encouragement and suggestions were so valuable. I appreciate the time and wisdom you shared with me.

A very heartfelt thanks to Christy Distler and Kaylena Radcliff for your encouragement, editing skills, and friendship. I knew I could count on either of you whenever I had a problem or question (or couldn't keep my tenses straight)!

To all the survivors who have shared their stories with me, thank you for your courage and for trusting me with your hearts.

I am so thankful for Doug, my amazing husband, that I could never thank enough. Thirty-six years ago, the first time I shared in public that I had been abused, he said, "You should be a professional speaker." I laughed. Without his love, encouragement, and support, I would never be able to write and speak, especially on this topic. He has been steady, calming, sympathetic, and okay with me crying into his chest—sometimes the moment he walks through the door. He is the best gift God has given me!

I am thankful to God for entrusting me with my story of sexual abuse and allowing me the privilege of walking with others through their stories. He has shown me more of his heart with each story, turning despair and ugliness to joy and beauty.

Let me know how this study has impacted you or your Bible study group or book club. I leave you with one more verse: Romans 8:31. "What then shall we say to these things? If God is for us, who can be against us?"

May God richly bless you!

End Notes

1. Dane Ortlund, *Gentle and Lowly: The Heart of Christ for Sinners and Sufferers* (Crossway, 2020), 159.

2. Mary York, "The God Who Sees: A look at abuse in the narrative of Hagar," Modern Reformation, March 25, 2022, accessed September 3, 2024, https://www.modernreformation.org/resources/articles/the-god-who-sees-a-look-at-abuse-in-the-narrative-of-hagar.

3. Karen Shogren, "LLV8: Equipping Organizations to Respond to and Prevent Sexual Harm," Levanta La Voz, 2023, 12.

4. Ibid.

5. York, "The God Who Sees: A look at abuse in the narrative of Hagar."

6. Joni Eareckson Tada, *The Practice of the Presence of Jesus* (Multnomah, 2023), 5.

7. Lynsey M. Barron, Esq., William P. Eiselstein, Esq., "Report of Independent Investigation into Sexual Misconduct of Ravi Zacharias," (Miller & Martin PLLC, February 9, 2021).

8. Scot McKnight and Laura Barringer, *A Church Called Tov: Forming a Goodness Culture That Resists Abuses of Power and Promotes Healing* (Tyndale Momentum, 2020), 17.

9. You can view the painting with this link: http://commons.wikimedia.org/wiki/File:Jean_Bourdichon_(French_-_Bathsheba_Bathing_-_Google_Art_Project.jpg

10. David T. Lamb, *Prostitutes and Polygamists: A Look at Love, Old Testament Style* (Zondervan, 2015), 130.

11. Ibid., 32.

12. John Piper, Ask Pastor John – Desiring God podcast, Episode 1735, January 24, 2022

13. Diane Mandt Langberg, PhD, *Counseling Survivors of Sexual Abuse* (Xulon Press, 2003), 45–51.

14. Mary DeMuth, *We Too: How the Church Can Respond Redemptively to the Sexual Abuse Crisis* (Harvest House, 2019), 11.

15. DeMuth, We Too, 71.

16. Derek Thomas, "Romans 8," Ligonier, accessed September 11, 2024, https://www.ligonier.org/learn/series/romans-8?utm_campaign=about&utm_source=connect.ligonier&utm_medium=referral&utm_content=romans-8.

17. Ortlund, *Gentle and Lowly*, 42.

18. Tommy Wasserman, "Does the Woman Caught in Adultery Belong in the Bible?," Text & Canon Institute, February 8, 2022, https://textandcanon.org/does-the-woman-caught-in-adultery-belong-in-the-bible/.

19. Ortlund, *Gentle and Lowly*, 96.

20. Griffin Paul Jackson, "The Top Reasons Young People Drop Out of Church," Christianity Today, January 15, 2019, www.christianitytoday.com.

21. "Statement from R. Albert Mohler Jr. on Sovereign Grace Churches," The Southern Baptist Theological Seminary, February 15, 2019, https://www.sbts.edu/news/statement-r-albert-mohler-jr-sovereign-grace-churches/.

22. McKnight and Barringer, *A Church Called TOV*, 44–45.

23. DeMuth, *We Too*, 73.

Bibliography

Barron, Lynsey M., Esq., and William P. Eiselstein, Esq. "Report of Independent Investigation into Sexual Misconduct of Ravi Zacharias." Miller & Martin PLLC, February 9, 2021.

Bourdichon, Jean. "Bathsheba Bathing." Painting, in the public domain. http://commons.wikimedia.org/wiki/File:Jean_Bourdichon_(French_-_Bathsheba_Bathing_-_Google_Art_Project.jpg.

DeMuth, Mary. *We Too: How the Church Can Respond Redemptively to the Sexual Abuse Crisis*. Harvest House, 2019.

Jackson, Griffin Paul. "The Top Reasons Young People Drop Out of Church." *Christianity Today*, January 15, 2019. www.christianitytoday.com.

Lamb, David T. *Prostitutes and Polygamists: A Look at Love, Old Testament Style*. Zondervan, 2015.

Langberg, Diane Mandt, PhD. *Counseling Survivors of Sexual Abuse*. Xulon Press, 2003.

Maier, Brian, PhD. *Forgiveness and Justice: A Christian Approach*. Kregel Publications, 2017.

McKnight, Scot, and Laura Barringer. *A Church Called Tov: Forming a Goodness Culture That Resists Abuses of Power and Promotes Healing*. Tyndale Momentum, 2020.

Mohler, R. Albert Jr. "Statement from R. Albert Mohler Jr. on Sovereign Grace Churches." The Southern Baptist Theological Seminary, February 15, 2019. https://www.sbts.edu/news/statement-r-albert-mohler-jr-sovereign-grace-churches/.https://www.sbts.edu/news/statement-r-albert-mohler-jr-sovereign-grace-churches/.

Ortlund, Dane. *Gentle and Lowly: The Heart of Christ for Sinners and Sufferers*. Crossway, 2020.

Piper, John. Ask Pastor John – Desiring God podcast. Episode 1735, January 24, 2022.

Radcliff, Lisa J. *"Hidden with Christ: Breaking Free from the Grip of Your Past"*. Book Baby, 2018.

Shogren, Karen. "LLV8: Equipping Organizations to Respond to and Prevent Sexual Harm." Levanta La Voz, 2023. Visit levantalavoz.com.

Tada, Joni Eareckson. *The Practice of the Presence of Jesus*. Multnomah, 2023.

Thomas, Derek. "Romans 8." Ligonier, accessed September 11, 2024. https://www.ligonier.org/learn/series/romans-8?utm_campaign=about&utm_source=connect.ligonier&utm_medium=referral&utm_content=romans-8.

Wasserman, Tommy. "Does the Woman Caught in Adultery Belong in the Bible?" Text & Canon Institute, February 8, 2022. https://textandcanon.org/does-the-woman-caught-in-adultery-belong-in-the-bible/.

York, Mary. "The God Who Sees: A look at abuse in the narrative of Hagar." Modern Reformation, March 25, 2022, accessed September 3, 2024. https://www.modernreformation.org/resources/articles/the-god-who-sees-a-look-at-abuse-in-the-narrative-of-hagar.

About the Author

Lisa J. Radcliff is an award-winning author, speaker, and certified mental health coach with more than thirty years of ministry experience. A survivor of childhood sexual abuse, Lisa is passionate about helping others discover healing through a deeper understanding of God's love and character. Her workshops, books, and Bible studies offer hope, humor, and spiritual insight for those navigating emotional wounds and faith-based recovery.

Lisa leads support groups for survivors and serves as a trainer for churches and ministries seeking to prevent abuse and respond with compassion. Her trauma-informed approach and biblical grounding make her a trusted voice in both ministry and mental health circles.

Lisa lives in Pennsylvania with her husband of more than forty years. They enjoy spending time with their three adult sons, nine grandchildren, and a steady stream of Seeing Eye® puppies in training. When not writing or speaking, Lisa loves quilting, cooking, rollercoasters, and cheering for the Philadelphia Eagles.

Lisa is available for speaking engagements and workshops. To connect, please visit lisajradcliff.com.